PENGUIN BOOKS
KHUSHWANT SINGH'S BIG FAT JOKE BOOK

Khushwant Singh was born in 1915 in Hadali,
Punjab. He was educated at Government College,
Lahore and at King's College and the Inner
Temple in London. He practiced at the Lahore
High Court for several years before joining the
Indian Ministry of External Affairs in 1947. He
began a distinguished career as a journalist with
All India Radio in 1951. Since then he has been
founder-editor of *Yojna* (1951-1953), editor of the
Illustrated Weekly of India (1979-1980), chief editor
of *New Delhi* (1979-1980), and editor of the
Hindustan Times (1980-1983). Today he is India's
best-known columnist and journalist.

Khushwant Singh has also had an extremely
successful career as a writer. Among the works he
has published are a classic two-volume history of
the Sikhs, several novels (the best known of
which are *Delhi*, *Train to Pakistan* and *The Company
of Women*), and a number of translated works and
non-fiction books on Delhi, nature and current
affairs.

Khushwant Singh was Member of Parliament
from 1980-1986. Among other honours he was

awarded the Padma Bhushan in 1974 by the President of India (he returned the decoration in 1984 in protest against the Union Government's siege of the Golden Temple, Amritsar).

KHUSHWANT SINGH'S

Big FAT joke book

PENGUIN BOOKS

In association with

VISION BOOKS

PENGUIN BOOKS
Published by the Penguin Group
Penguin Books India Pvt Ltd, 11 Community Centre, Panchsheel Park, New
Delhi 110 017, India
Penguin Group (USA) Inc., 375 Hudson Street, New York, New York 10014,
USA
Penguin Group (Canada), 90 Eglinton Avenue East, Suite 700, Toronto,
Ontario, M4P 2Y3, Canada (a division of Pearson Penguin Canada Inc.)
Penguin Books Ltd, 80 Strand, London WC2R 0RL, England
Penguin, Ireland, 25 St Stephen's Green, Dublin 2, Ireland (a division of
Penguin Books Ltd)
Penguin Group (Australia), 250 Camberwell Road, Camberwell, Victoria
3124, Australia (a division of Pearson Australia Group Pty Ltd)
Penguin Group (NZ), cnr Airborne and Rosedale Roads, Albany, Auckland
1310, New Zealand (a division of Pearson New Zealand Ltd)
Penguin Group (South Africa) (Pty) Ltd, 24 Sturdee Avenue, Rosebank,
Johannesburg 2196, South Africa

Penguin Books Ltd, Registered Offices: 80 Strand, London WC2R 0RL, England

First published by Penguin Books India 2000

The jokes in this volume were previously published as part of
Khushwant Singh's Joke Books Vols. 1–5

Copyright © Mala Dayal 2000

Illustrations by Samapti

All rights reserved

10 9

Typeset in Casablanca by SÜRYA, New Delhi
Printed at Baba Barkhanath Printers, New Delhi

Acknowledgements

Grateful acknowledgement is made to the following who contributed some of these jokes:

M.M Kapoor, New Delhi; Suddha Basu, New Delhi; Vijay Gakkhar; Mahendra Kumar Rekhi, Rourkela; Mr Hadi, Chittagong, Bangladesh; R.R. Bajaj, New Delhi; S.N.K Naidu, Sidhouti; Reeten Ganguly, Tejpur; K.R. Prithvi Raj, Mumbai; Tushar, Najibabad; Tushar Kumar; Kamaljit Singh Ahluwalia, Amritsar; K.S. Menon, Mumbai; Ajay Sood, Delhi; H.S. Rattan; Shridhar Vyas, Bangalore; R.K. Murthi; Mukhtiar Singh Bhatia, Jamshedpur; Satindra Singh; Siddhantamangal; Kashyap, Guwahati; Vijay Dawar, Faridabad; J.P. Singh Kaka, New Delhi; R. Ravi, Bangalore; Debashish Bose, Calcutta; Vineet Khanna, Chandigarh; R.P.D. Sud, Ludhiana; A. Manjunath, Bangalore; Lysondra D'Mello, Bombay; J.S. Arora, Calcutta; Maasonna Rifaqat Ali, New Delhi; Rajeshwari Singh, New Delhi; Jyotica Sikand, New Delhi; G.C. Bhandari, Meerut; Hardip Kaur Sandhu, Denmark; Amrit Kachru, Washington DC; S.R. Patnaik, Cuttack; Anirban Sen, New Delhi; S. Parmeswaran, USA; H.S. Jatana, Mohali; Channi Pantal, New Delhi; V. Lalith Prasad,

Hyderabad; Vikas Kaushik, New Delhi; Sucharita Das Sharma, Calcutta; S. Vishwanath, Mandya; P.S. Romesh, Bangalore; Gurpreet Singh, New Agra; P.P. Jacob, Kottayam; Thomas D' Mello, Kundapara; Prof. Raja Ram Mehrotra, U.C. Hakeem, Bareilly; Kaushik and Kanishka Datta, Calcutta; Sudheendra Bani, Bangalore; Shashank Shekhar, New Bombay; T.T. Subhashini, Ahmedabad; Rajan Sharma, Mukerian; R.S. Dutta, Chandigarh; P.V. Nayak, New Delhi; Ashish Saxena, New Delhi; Dara C. Shroff, Bangalore; S.K. Rana, Meerut; Dr R. Venkataraman, East Sussex, England; N. Anantaramn, Bangalore; Prakash Chaudhary, Lucknow; Harjeet Kaur, New Delhi; B.D. Desai, Surat; R.A. Goswami, Warangal; Deepanjan Basu, New Delhi; G.B. Anil, Chennai; Amir C. Tuteja, Washington DC; Gaurav Marwaha, Rajpura; Rizwan Vasser, Calcutta; S.B. Iyer, Bangalore; Baldev Kapur, Delhi; Vijay Kayal, Hojai; Anupam and Pranav Anshumati, Patna; A.P. Gibbs, Hyderbad; Raj Bir Singh, Calcutta; Sham Keswani, New Delhi; Mehtab Ali, Amrohi; Saket Budhiraja, New Delhi; Rose Sands; Firoz Bakht Ahmed, Delhi; Ashish Bakshi, New Delhi; Veerashwar Sobti, New Delhi;Tara Baswani, New Delhi; Tara Baswani, New Delhi; Judson K. Cornelius, Hyderabad.

An American delegation on a visit to India were being shown round the capital. In the evening they were taken to the Secretariat for a panoramic view of Vijay Chowk and Rajpath. Came the closing hour and thousands upon thousands of clerks poured out of their offices. The place was crammed with bicycles and pedestrians.

'Who are all these people?' asked the leader of the American delegation.

'They are the common people of India; the real rulers of the country,' proudly replied the minister accompanying the visitors.

A few minutes later came a fleet of flag-bearing limousines escorted by pilots on motorcycles followed by jeeps full of armed policemen. 'And who are these?' asked the American.

'These are us,' replied the minister with the same pride, 'the servants of the people.'

❐

God and Satan got into an argument over the repairs of the wall dividing heaven and hell. God insisted that all the damage was caused by people in hell and so Satan should pay for its repair. Satan was adamant that they should share the cost. When they failed to resolve their dispute, Satan said: 'Let's appoint an arbitrator and let our lawyers argue the case before him.'

'I don't mind having an arbitrator,' replied God, 'but you will have an advantage over me. I have no lawyers in heaven; they are all on your side.'

Two men met in heaven. 'What did you die of?' asked the one.

'I died of extreme cold. And what about you?'

'I came home from work and thought I heard my wife talking to a stranger. On entering the house, I searched every nook and corner but could not find anyone anywhere. I felt so guilty of my suspicion that my heart failed.'

Hearing this, the other one said, 'Had you cared to open the fridge, neither of us would have died.'

❐

A Hindu family living in a village near the Indo-Pak border which was often visited by Khalistani terrorists, decided to migrate to another Indian state. Their Sikh neighbours came to bid them a tearful farewell. One of them noticed that the head of the Hindu family put the picture of Sant Jarnail Singh Bhindranwale into his trunk. 'Why are you taking Bhindranwale's picture with you?' he asked. The Hindu replied with tears in his eyes, 'Whenever I miss my *vatan* (birthplace) I will look at it and feel how lucky I am to have got away.'

❐

A vice-chancellor died and was received at the gates of paradise for questioning before his fate could be decided. 'What were you doing when you were on earth?' asked Dharamraj.

'I was vice-chancellor of a university.'

'I see. You've suffered the pangs of hell on earth and deserve a break in paradise.'

The next arrival was put through the same questioning. 'I was vice-chancellor of a university for three successive terms,' he replied.

'Put him in hell,' ordered Dharamraj. 'He's got into the habit.'

⌐

Yahya Khan, trying to persuade a yokel to volunteer for the Pakistani Air Force, took him inside the aircraft and explained: 'You press this yellow button and the engine will start. Then you press the red one and the plane will take off. It is all very simple.'

'But how do I bring the plane down?' asked the yokel, puzzled.

'You don't have to bother about that,' explained Yahya Khan. 'Leave that to the Indian Air Force.'

❐

Vietnamese girls were the GIs' top favourites during the American military presence in the Vietnam war. 'They can be poor in history, but really great on dates,' Leo Shaw assures us in his book entitled *Confucius Say*. Don't be misled by their being bow-legged: 'Just because their legs are like ice-tongs, does not mean they are frigid.' Their being poorly endowed in the way of busts became the GIs' favourite joke. 'As one falsie said to another, let's pack up and leave her flat.'

Next to getting venereal disease it was having a pregnant girl on his hands that was the GI's nightmare. The pill was not known and abortions risky. Hence the description of an optimist in Vietnam was one who rubbed vanishing cream on his girlfriend's tummy hoping the bulge would disappear. The sanest advice this American Confucius could give the randy GI was, 'Women over forty best; they don't yell, don't tell, don't swell and are grateful as hell.'

❏

'They say Pakistanis are prospecting for oil in Sindh and Punjab. Is that true?'
'Yes. But not to get petrol to run motor

cars. Only grease for the palms of politicians and ministers.'

❐

A gentleman travelled all the way from Islamabad to Karachi to have an aching tooth taken out. The Karachi dentist said, 'Surely you have dentists in Islamabad! You did not have to come all this way to have your teeth attended to.'

'We have no choice. In Islamabad we are not allowed to open our mouths,' replied the man with the aching tooth.

❐

An American tourist to India hired a

Sardarji guide to take him around Delhi and Agra. When taken to Agra Fort, he admired the architecture and asked how many years it took to build. The Sardarji replied, 'Twenty years.' The American remarked, 'You Indians are a lazy lot. In America, this could have been built in five years.' At the Taj the American again admired its beauty and asked how many years it had taken to build. The Sardarji reduced the period considerably and replied, 'Only ten years, sir.' The American retorted: 'Didn't I say you Indians are slow workers! In America, we can construct such buildings in two-and-a-half years.' It was the same story everywhere. The American admired the architecture but criticized the construction period. The Sardarji finally got irritated. When the taxi was nearing Qutab Minar, the American asked: 'What is that tower?' Came the

reply, 'Sir, I'll have to go and find out. When I was passing this way last evening, there was nothing there.'

❒

Meetha Mal Goel who has a *halwa* business in our locality went to consult advocate Hoshiar Mal on a legal problem. '*Vakeel* sahib, a dog ran into my shop and before I could shoo it away he took a mouthful of halwa from the big plate. I had to throw the rest away. The *halwa* was worth at least Rs 50. Please tell me if I can recover my money from the owner of the dog.'

'Most certainly you can,' assured the *vakeel* sahib. 'The master of the dog is responsible for what his dog does.'

'That is very good,' said Meetha Mal Goel. 'Please let me have fifty rupees since it was your dog that ate my *halwa*.'

❏

The broilers and eggs of a poultry breeder were the best in the market. A man complimented him and asked: 'What do you feed your birds to get such excellent products?'

'The very best food: almonds, pistachios and pure ghee mixed in the chicken feed,' answered the proud breeder.

'How interesting!' replied the other. 'I am from the income tax department. I'd like to know where you got all the money to buy such an expensive diet.'

Thereafter the breeder was on guard.

When the next visitor complimented him on his produce and asked, 'What do you give your birds to eat?' He replied, 'Nothing, nothing at all. I starve them.'

'That calls for action,' replied the visitor. 'I am from the Society for the Prevention of Cruelty to Animals. I charge you with the offence of starving chickens.'

When a third visitor came and made similar inquiries, the breeder was more cautious in his reply. 'I give them fifty paise each everyday and let them buy what they like to eat,' he said.

❏

Indian VIPs on the hit list have been sent an elaborate set of do's and don'ts to elude terrorists on their trail. Of these the most important instructions are not to follow a regular routine but vary their timings and change their habits often as possible, e.g. don't go for your morning or evening walk at the same time to the same park, don't go to the same hotel or restaurant every day etc. To these precautions, a wit who knows the habits of Indian politicians added: 'Don't sleep in the same bed with the same person every night.'

❐

A fourth son was born in the home of a minister's family. The father invited his Sardarji friend to join in the celebrations and choose a name for the newborn child. 'What names have you given to the three elder boys?' asked the Sardarji.

'One is Rahmat Elahi (by God's kindness), the second Barkat Elahi (by God's grace) and the third Mahbub Elahi (beloved of God),' replied the proud father.

The Sardarji pondered over the names for a while and replied, 'I suggest you name your fourth son, Bas Kar Elahi (God, that is enough).'

❏

A couple hired a new chauffeur. The memsahib asked him to take her out for shopping and was very shaken by the experience. Back home, she pleaded with her husband, 'Please dear, you must sack this new chauffeur at once. He is so rash he nearly killed me three times this morning.'

'Darling, don't be so hasty,' replied the husband, 'give him another chance.'

❑

A grey-bearded Sardarji was asked how his family was doing. 'Nothing to complain,' he replied, stroking his long beard. 'Akaal Purukh (God) has been very good to us. I have three sons. The eldest is a lawyer, the second is a doctor, the third a lecturer in a college.'

'That's very good. And Sardar sahib, you must be enjoying your days of retirement.'

'No retirement-shitirement for me,' protested the grey-beard. 'I ply my taxi. How else could I manage to support my sons and their families?'

This happened when I met Dev Anand. His chauffeur had gone off to get a bite. We sat in the lobby of the Oberoi Sheraton awaiting his return. Groups of people collected at a respectable distance to gaze at their idol. All I could hear was a hum of 'Dev Anand's. Then someone asked somewhat loudly: 'Who is the Sardar with him?'

And someone replied: 'Don't know. Must be one of his chamchas.'

❐

A Haryanavi peasant was walking down the road carrying a heavy sack of grain on his head. A kind Sardar farmer drawing his bullock cart offered him a lift. The Haryanavi gratefully accepted the offer and sat down in the cart but kept the sack on his head.

'Chaudhury, why don't you put down the sack in the *gadda*?'

'Sardarji,' replied the Haryanavi, 'your cart is already heavily loaded. I don't want to put more burden on your poor bullock.'

❐

A rich lady had four children, all of whom turned out to be very bright. She was always boasting of their records at school and was sure that when they grew up they would bring credit to India. I asked her somewhat sarcastically if she had ever heard of the family planning slogan *Hum do hamaarey do*. 'Yes,' she replied somewhat haughtily, 'that is for the *aira ghaira-hoi polloi*—not for people like us who have highly intelligent children and can afford to give them the best education.'

'In that case why don't you have five more and give India another *nau ratans–* nine gems?'

She ignored my sarcasm and replied: 'I have just read a book on population statistics. It says that every fifth child born in the world is a Chinese.'

❒

In the gossip room of both Houses of Parliament, besides reputations of politicians being torn up, some good anecdotes are manufactured. This one is about Babu Jagjivan Ram's reactions to the new cabinet ministers appointed by Rajiv Gandhi.

Question: 'Babuji, do you think new ministers like K.R. Narayanan and Natwar Singh, who have spent most of their years in foreign countries or in aircooled offices in the secretariat, know enough about the countryside to be effective?'

Answer: 'No, I think they should spend some time in India's villages to get to know villagers' problems.'

Question: 'In that case, don't you think Mr Rajiv Gandhi should also spend some time acquainting himself with villagers' problems?'

Answer: 'No, he does not need to do so. He is well-acquainted with them. He knows the Asiad Village.'

❒

When Sir Bertrand Glancy was governor of the Punjab and nearing retirement, Sir Stafford Cripps, who was staying with him at Government House, tried to pull his leg about the very different standard of living he would soon have to get used to in England. Cripps comment was, 'Well, Glancy, you'll have to black your own boots when you get home.' Sir Bertrand, without a flicker of a smile, replied, 'Oh no! I'm going to Kenya where I can boot my own blacks.'

❐

It is said that a team of researchers studying the sexual habits of city-dwellers interviewed a cross-section of Mumbai's business community. Among the questions posed to them, one was: What do you do immediately after you have had sex? The answers were most revealing. Ten per cent replied that they simply went to sleep. Another 10 per cent replied that they washed themselves and took some nourishment—a glass of fruit juice, aerated water or a sandwich. The remaining 80 per cent, after much cajoling, replied: 'Then we go home.'

❐

A swankily dressed and opinionated young man got into a noisy, crowded bus. With a very superior air he remarked to the conductor: 'You seem to have collected all the animals from the zoo in your bus.' A passenger retorted: 'Sir, not all of them were in the bus till you got on. A donkey was missing.'

❐

A Hindu, a Muslim and a Sikh were discussing the marvellous achievements of their own brands of surgery. Said the Hindu, 'I know of a *vaidji* who joined a severed arm with the use of Ayurvedic glue. You can't even tell where the arm had been cut.' Not to be outdone, the Muslim spoke: 'A *hakeem* sahib has evolved a new kind of adhesive ointment. He used it on a fellow who had his head cut off. You can't tell where the neck was severed.' It was now the Sardarji's turn to extol the latest developments in Sikh surgery. 'We have gone much further,' he said thumping his chest proudly. 'There was this *chacha* of mine who was cut into two around his navel. Our Sikh surgeon immediately slaughtered a goat and joined its rear half to my *chacha's* upper half. So we have our *chacha* as well as two litres of milk every day.'

❏

During one of my periodic bouts with the *Times* (London) crossword puzzles, my eye fell on a St Valentine message printed alongside. There were six full columns with almost a hundred professings of love in each column. I was disappointed to find what little progress lovers had made in expressing their affection. More than 500 messages said no more than the three words, 'I love you', or repeated the old doggerel: 'Roses are red, violets are blue, Dizzie darling, I love you.' A fair proportion could not even do that and exhausted themselves in a series of Xs, presumably expressing desire for labial contact. There were many which were totally inane, to wit: '*Hee hee tee hee hee turn tee, did I say I love you?*' And: 'Heffalumpus for breakfast, Heffalumpus for tea, Heffalumpus for ever, when this week you marry me.' Lots use private language: 'Baby bear loves horrid hedgepig.'

Indian emigrants have also found entry in England's love letters. One addressed to Shrimati reads: 'You sweet *gulab jamun* of my most delectable dreams! If you don't know what to do, lie back and think of your Indian juice.'

Two very drunk Punjabis were returning home on a bicycle from the *theka*. On the way the man on the carrier fell off; the other cycled on. When he got home he found his companion missing. He cycled back towards the *theka* to find his friend sitting calmly in the middle of the road. The cyclist dismounted and asked gently: 'You OK?' 'I am fine,' replied the other, 'it is a comfortable carrier seat; keep pedalling unless you are tired.'

❏

This one comes from the Delhi University campus and is based on the two meanings of the Hindi word *maang* which can mean both demand and the parting in the hair. Students of a girls' college took out a procession to protest against living conditions in their hostel. They divided themselves in two groups. One shouted *hamaaree maangey*, the second lot replied *pooree karo*. So they went round the campus asking for their demands to be met.

The procession wound its way past a boys' college. The cheerleaders shouted: *Hamaaree maangey*. Before the second batch of girls could reply, the boys shouted back *sindhoor sey bharo*—(fill them with vermilion powder).

❏

'Papa, what is the name of the Indian woman who reached the top of Everest?' asked a boy. 'I have to prepare for my General Knowledge paper.'

His father scratched his head and replied: 'I am sorry, her name escapes me.'

'What was the name of the other Indian astronaut who did not go up with Rakesh Sharma?' the boy asked again.

The father again looked blank and replied: 'I don't know.'

'Then tell me the names of the Indians who have won the Nobel Prize.'

'Sorry,' replied the father. 'I can't answer that one either.'

Seeing the look of disappointment on his son's face he added: 'But you must keep asking questions. If you don't ask, how will you ever learn anything?'

❒

A firm of solicitors in Mumbai go under

the name of Patel, Patel, Patel and Patel. The office phone rang and the voice at the other end asked:

'May I speak to Mr Patel?'

'Mr Patel is not in his seat.'

'In that case can I speak to the other Mr Patel?'

'The other Mr Patel is out of station.'

'Then put me on to the third Mr Patel.'

'Sorry, the third Mr Patel has gone out for lunch.'

'Okay then, I will speak to the last Mr Patel.'

'Patel speaking.'

❒

A patriotic Sardarji saw the Indian tricolour fluttering in the breeze. He stood

at attention and saluted. 'Why did you salute that flag?' asked a passerby. 'It has saffron for the Hindus, green for the Muslims and white for all the others. Nothing for the Sikhs.'

Pat came the Sardarji's reply: 'And what do you think the *danda* on which the flag flutters represents? Only the Sikhs.'

❑

An elderly and rich bania who was mean in money matters acquired a young, pretty wife who was a spendthrift. He thought of a scheme to teach his wife the habit of saving. He presented her with a small tin box with a slit in its lid, locked it and put the key in his pocket. 'Meyree jaan,' he said to her, 'every time you let me kiss you, I will put a four anna piece into the box. At the end of the month I will unlock it. All the money in it will be yours to spend as you like.'

The scheme worked very well. The young wife showed more willingness to be kissed and her elderly husband was quite happy to part with four anna coins for what he got in return.

At the end of the month with a grand gesture he produced the key from his pocket and unlocked the box. What he saw did not please him. There were many fifty paise and rupee coins in the box. 'Where did these come from?' he demanded angrily. 'I've only been putting in chavannis.'

'Not everyone is as mean as you,' replied the wife saucily.

American astronauts land on the moon only to find Russians awaiting to greet them. They are comparing notes when they see a family of Sikhs strolling by. 'When did you people get to the moon?' ask the Yanks and the Ruskies.

'Many years ago,' replies the Sardarji blandly. 'We came here after the Partition.'

❑

A newly appointed health minister of a northern state (guess which?) whose knowledge of English was somewhat elementary was on his first official visit to the largest hospital in the Capital. The Director of Medical Services took the minister round the operating theatres and general wards till they came to the women patients' section. 'This, sir, is the labour ward,' explained the director. The minister stopped in his tracks and said firmly: 'I will not visit this ward. Don't you know we have a labour minister in the government? I must not trespass into his domain.'

❐

Mr T.A. Pai, a former cabinet minister, when asked to comment on the 'no-change' in the style of functioning and the poor performance of the Janata government, is said to have remarked: 'Why should anyone have expected anything better from them? They are only our B team.'

❐

A well-dressed gentleman hurrying along the road was stopped by an acquaintance. 'My friend,' said the man, sotto voce, 'I must draw your attention to the fact that your fly-buttons are undone.'

'I know,' replied the well-dressed man, brushing aside his acquaintance. 'I am on my way to the Income Tax office to make a voluntary disclosure.'

A party of American pressmen were granted an interview with Chairman Mao Tse-tung. After having heard the denunciation of the Soviet Union and other imperialist powers, one of the party asked the Chairman: 'Sir, what in your opinion would have happened if, instead of John

F. Kennedy, Mr Khrushchev had been assassinated?'

Chairman Mao pondered over the question for a while before he replied, 'I doubt very much if Aristotle Onassis would have married Mrs Khrushchev.'

❐

Tarlochan Singh of Markfed pumps me with the wonderful achievements of his organization. He thrusts a large parcel of Markfed products on me: canned fruit and vegetables, fruit juices, jams, pickles and the Punjabi manna—*sarson ka saag*. 'We are exporting our *saag* all over the world,' he states with evident pride. 'You try it out when you are in Mumbai; there is nothing like it.' There is certainly nothing like it: half a tin consumed will produce enough gas in your belly to make you airborne like a jet plane.

❒

A Sardarji is lying across the rail tracks with a bottle of whisky and a tandoori chicken within reach. A passerby asks: 'Sardarji, why are you lying on the rail lines? A train may come any moment and run over you.'

'Precisely!' answers the Sardarji. 'I have no desire to live any longer. I want to kill myself.'

'Then why have you this bottle of liquor and the tandoori chicken beside you?'

'Why not?' demands the Sardarji. 'You

can't rely on trains running on time any more. You don't expect me to die of hunger and thirst, do you?'

❏

This happened during the British Raj. The then sub-collector of Penugonda (now in Andhra Pradesh) and his memsahib were always quarrelling. One night the Burra sahib became very angry with his wife and yelled, 'You bloody bitch! I will slice you in two.' At that precise moment a drunken gentleman who was passing by the bungalow shouted, 'Please let me have the bottom half.'

❏

A Mrs D. Thomas of Guwahati put in an advertisement in the *Assam Tribune* of 17 July 1985 for the sale of her cottage, land and a pair of oxen. It is not known whether it was the lady or the compositor of the paper who was responsible for the ad that ultimately appeared prominently boxed. It read as follows: 'For sale. Five *bighas* of high land adjacent to NH 37, 20 km from Guwahati city on the way to Sonapur, with a small cottage, electricity, deep tubewell with electric pump, cowshed and a pain of bullach.'

❒

P resident Zia-ul-Haq's trusted barber seemed to have become infected by the popular demand for the restoration of democracy. One morning while clipping the President's hair he asked: '*Gareeb pur war*! When are you going to have elections in Pakistan?'

The President ignored the question with the contempt it deserved from a military dictator. At the next hair-cutting session, the barber asked: '*Aali jah*! Isn't it time you redeemed your promise to hold elections?'

The President controlled his temper and remained silent.

On the third hair-clipping session, the barber again blurted out: '*Banda Nawaz*, the *awam* (common people) are clamouring for elections, when will you order them?'

The President could not contain himself anymore and exploded: '*Gaddar*! I will have you taught a lesson you will never forget.' And ordered his minions to take away the barber and give him ten lashes on his buttocks.

The barber fell at the great man's feet and whined: '*Zill-i-Illahi* (shadow of God), I eat your salt; how can I become a *gaddar* (traitor)? I only mentioned elections to make my job easier.'

'What do you mean?' demanded Zia-ul-Haq.

'Every time I utter the word election, Your Excellency's hair stands on end and is much easier to clip.'

❐

Dr S.K. Kulshrestha teaching in D.A.V. College, Dehradun, has sent me two examples of the language communication gap which he encountered. Since Dehradun is not far from Punjab, many

Punjabis seek admission to his college. However, since preference is given to UP boys and girls, outsiders are asked to state their 'length of residence in UP', and attach their certificates. A boy from a Punjab village filled in his form and against the column 'length of residence' wrote, '366 kilometres'.

Another applicant filling in details of his name, address etc. put against the column 'born' the simple reply: 'Yes.'

❏

A greenhorn not familiar with the manners of the city folk happened to be spending his holidays with his uncle in Lucknow. During his stay there was a death in the neighbouring house. The uncle decided to take his nephew along to the bereaved family to offer his condolences. In proper Lucknavi style the uncle began to extol the virtues of the dead man: 'He was a great soul. He was not only your *chachaji* but the *chachaji* of our entire *mohalla*. May his soul rest in peace! We will miss him as long as we live.' And so on. Our greenhorn maintained a stiff-lipped silence.

Back home, the uncle reprimanded his nephew, 'Don't they teach you manners at home? You also should have said something about the dead man being like your own *chachaji*.'

The lad apologized saying he had never been to condolence meetings with anyone but would bear the advice in mind.

A few weeks later a friend of the greenhorn lost his wife and he decided to offer his condolences in the formula prescribed: 'She was a great soul. She was not only your wife, but the wife of all of us in our *mohalla*.'

☐

The late Bhulabhai Desai was renowned for his ready wit which helped him to score over his adversaries in debate. Less is known of an equally witty and resourceful person, Sri N.N. Sarkar who happened to be the law minister before Independence. Sarkar was introducing a bill to make provisions for the care of illegitimate children and mistresses who were left unprovided by men they had lived with. Desai thought he would put Sarkar on the spot by asking: 'May I know from the hon'ble law minister what is his government's attitude towards men keeping mistresses?'

N.N. Sarkar was quick to retort: 'Sir, we have no first-hand experience of such relationships and will be happy to receive guidance from honourable members like yourself who have more knowledge and experience of the subject.'

❐

Since the army is gradually taking over more and more functions of the police, there is much heartburning in police circles. A constable who could not take the reduction of his status much longer, got talking to a jawan: 'Bhai, I am told that you jawans of the army have to spend many years on the borders before you get leave. Meanwhile, your wives go on bearing children. Is this really true? How do you treat these ready-made children planted on you?'

The jawan replied cooly: 'I do not think this is a common occurrence. But when it takes place we enrol these ready-made children, as you call them, into the police.'

❐

Not to be outdone by Rakesh Sharma and Ravish Malhotra, two sturdy Punjabis applied to NASA, the American space agency, to be taken to outer space. Their application was accepted and they were asked to report at the centre in California. They were told that during their period of training they must not take any alcohol. They followed the strict regimen imposed on them for several weeks, till one day they could not resist the temptation to wet their lips. Since no strong drink was available anywhere near their centre, they drank up a canister of rocket fuel. Next morning the following dialogue took place between them: 'This is your friend speaking. Have you been to the lavatory this morning?'

'No, why do you ask such a silly question?'

'If you haven't, don't try. I am speaking from Tokyo.'

❏

A certain gentleman from northern India built a house without a roof. When asked why he had not completed the job, he replied: 'Don't you know that the government has decided to put a ceiling on all urban property?'

❏

I am beholden to Ganga Saran Sinha for the following two anecdotes of Maulana Mohammed Ali, renowned nationalist leader and a great wit of his times. Ganga Babu assures me of their veracity.

The Maulana went to see how the central assembly functioned and got a pass to the visitors' gallery. At the time the presiding officer was Vithalbhai Patel. No sooner than he saw the Maulana enter the visitors' box, he stood up and announced to the members of the legislature: 'It is not customary for the presiding officer to take notice of any person, however eminent, in the visitors' gallery. However, I will break all conventions and say how honoured we are with the presence of Maulana Mohammed Ali. I hope it will not be long before we see him as an elected member in our midst rather than seated up in the visitors' gallery.'

The announcement was greeted with applause. The Maulana who had propagated the boycott of legislatures under British rule gracefully acknowledged the clapping with a bow and replied: 'I am much honoured by your reference to me but would prefer to stay where I am so that I can look down on all of you.'

On another occasion the Maulana who had received a doctorate from Al Azhar

University of Cairo decided to visit the Central Hall of Parliament in the *chogha* (gown) presented to him. It happened to look very much like a *burqa* and combined with the Maulana's flowing locks gave him a somewhat feminine appearance from the rear. In those times the Central Hall was equipped with a bar where drinks were available at very cheap rates. A somewhat inebriated member decided to have a crack at the Maulana. 'For a moment I thought we had the pleasure of Begum sahiba's company in our midst. From the rear you look exactly like a woman.'

'I am sorry to disappoint you,' retorted the Maulana, 'my wife would never agree to come to an assemblage of *hijdas*. I don't have any such inhibitions.'

❏

Three young women, a Tamilian, a Maharashtrian and a Punjaban happened to die on the same day and arrived in the office of Dharamraj, the keeper of life's records. He began with the Tamilian about her life. He first questioned her about her lifestyle. 'I have been very good; I was a virgin until I married and have been utterly faithful and dutiful to my husband. I looked after my mother-in-law and prayed everyday,' she said.

'That's very good. I will recommend you for first class accommodation in Paradise,' said Dharamraj.

The Maharashtrian came next. 'I was a full-blooded Maratha so I could not be quite as chaste in thought and deed as my Tamilian sister. But I didn't hurt anyone and I kept my husband happy,' she responded.

'For you, second class accommodation

in Paradise,' replied Dharamraj.

'And what about you?' he asked the lady from the Land of the Five Rivers.

'I was a very bad woman,' she replied. 'I did everything I shouldn't have done; I never said my prayers, I quarrelled with my *saas* (mother-in-law), and had an affair with my *devar* (husband's younger brother).'

'That was very bad, *behenjee*,' said Dharamraj.

'Do anything you like with me but don't call me your *behen*,' snapped the Punjaban.

'Okay! In that case you come to my apartment this evening.'

❑

Question: What is common between the

Indo-Pak border and postal envelopes
issued by the Indian Post Office?

Answer: Neither can be sealed.

❏

A number of well-wishers who called to
condole with me when my mother died
said they had come 'to condone' my
mother's death. Ma, forgive them for they
did not know what they said! They meant
well. As did my photographer friend T.S.
Nagarajan, who, whenever he wanted to
say he did something with deliberation
would say, 'I wantonly did.' There was
never anything wanton about Nagarajan;
he is as strait-laced a Tamil as I know.

Philip Norman of the *Times* (London)
has a new crop of malapropisms which I

had not heard of before. He writes of his grandmother's verbal gaffes. After visiting her sister in hospital she described the 'sirloin' drip attached to the patient's arm with doctor's 'hoovering' around and giving her 'the RIP treatment'.

Another lady working in a haunted house had to call in a priest to 'circumcise' (exorcise) the ghost. In a restaurant the excellence of the food served was ascribed to the chef who had earned a 'Condom Bleu' (Cordon Bleu or the blue ribbon awarded to the best of cooks).

Malapropisms did not end with Mrs Malaprop's description of a person being 'as headstrong as an allegory (alligator) on the banks of the Nile'. They continue to be as many-splendoured as 'all the colours of the rectum (spectrum).'

This anecdote is about two Indians settled in England. One had been living there for some years and had caught on the some of the quaint euphemisms of the English. The other, a recent settler, was as yet unaware of them. They were invited for dinner by their English friends. After they had their drinks, their hostess asked them, 'Would you like a wash before I serve dinner?' The knowledgeable one replied, 'No thanks.' The new settler replied, 'I washed my hands before I came.'

On their way back after dinner the older settler admonished his friend. 'My dear chap, in England "would you like a wash" does not mean "would you like to wash your hands". It is a polite way of asking would you like to urinate?' The new settler made a mental note of it. Some days later when he was invited by another English friend and after the drinks he was asked by his hostess, 'Would you like a wash, before I serve dinner?' He replied promptly, 'No thank you madam. I washed against a tree before coming to your house.'

❐

I reproduce the following excerpts of Churchill's wit sent in by Samiran Sarkar because I had never heard of them.

Sir William Joyson Hicks made some statement in Parliament to which Churchill gave signs of demurring. 'I see my right honourable friend shakes his head,' said Hicks, 'but I am only expressing my own opinion.' 'And I,' answered Churchill, 'am only shaking my own head.'

The genuineness of Churchill's joke about Sir Alfred Bossom's entry into the House has never been questioned. 'Bossom?' he said, 'What an extraordinary name . . . neither one thing nor the other.'

Once when his race horse Colonist II finished fourth Churchill had his own excuse. He said that he had a serious talk with the horse just before the race. 'I told him this is a very big race and if you win it you will never have to run again. You will spend the rest of your life in agreeable female company.'

Then Churchill added, 'Colonist II did not keep his mind on the race.'

When a General during the Second World War pompously asserted that 'putting the troops in the picture before a battle was the sort of familiarity which breeds contempt,' Churchill retorted: 'You know, General, without a certain amount of familiarity it is extraordinarily difficult to breed anything at all.'

Churchill's grandmother, the Duchess of Marlborough, had this to say on the arrival of her grandson:

'I have myself given birth to quite a number of infants. They were all pretty vocal when they arrived, but such an earth-shaking noise as this newborn baby made I have never heard.'

❏

V.K. Krishna Menon was a bachelor and hated people with large broods of children. In his early career as a barrister, a couple with three girls in tow called on him and suggested that he accompany them to a theatre as they had an extra ticket. The

sixsome waited for a bus and the first one
had only room for four (no overloading).
The second one came after five minutes
and had only three vacancies and the third
had two. So they decided to walk the
distance instead of being late for the show.

Menon with his walking stick was
tramping on the cobbled-stone pavement
and tuck-tuck-tucking. The father, already
irritated with not getting the bus,
remarked, 'Dammit, Krishna, can't you
put a piece of rubber at the end of your
stick?'

Pat came the reply: 'If you had put
one at the end of yours, we would have
got into a bus.'

❑

A man went into a bar and ordered a

drink. After he had finished and got up to leave, the bartender asked, 'What about the bill?'

'I have already paid,' he replied and left. Soon after, another man came in. He, too, ordered a drink, drank it and left saying that he had already paid.

The third customer came in. As he was drinking, the bartender told him, 'Before you two men came here, they ordered drinks and left, telling me that they had already paid. What do you think about that?'

'Stop arguing and return my change,' the man said.

❏

S.K. Singh, our ambassador in Islamabad,

has a gift of putting everyone at their ease. During a recent visit to Delhi he happened to call upon some friends who have a precocious five-year-old daughter. After having exchanged pleasantries. with his friends, SK felt he ought to talk to their daughter. In his most charming diplomatic manner he asked the child:

'Beta, what school do you go to?'

The child told him.

'And what are your favourite subjects?'

The child rattled off her favourite subjects.

More questions followed; and answers given. SK thought he had done his duty as a guest. The child decided it was her turn to ask questions.

'And Uncle, what do you do for a living?'

'I am an ambassador. Beta do you know what an ambassador is?'

The child nodded her head wisely and replied: 'Yes, Daddy has one.'

❏

A Punjabi matron emigrated to England taking her only son with her. She took to the country like a duck to water. But her boy missed his village and began to waste away. Ultimately the lady took the boy to the local doctor for a medical check-up.

'Does the boy eat well and sleep well?' asked the medico.

The lady replied in her Punjabi English: '*Na, na doctor sahib, na eatda, na saleepda; but weepda hee weepda.*'

❏

Kakey da Hotel is a very popular eating-place in Connaught Circus. It started off as a humble *Kakey da Dhaaba* with stools and charpaees laid out on the pavement and the tandoor, handees and pateelas placed in the open. With prosperity the kitchen went into the rear and a dining room was furnished with tables, chairs as well as a wash basin. One evening a patron having finished his meal went to rinse his mouth in the wash basin. He proceeded to do so with great vigour: gurgling, spitting and blowing his nose. This ruined the appetites of the other diners who protested to the proprietor. Kakaji went to the rinser-spitter and admonished him, 'Haven't you ever eaten in a good hotel before?'

'Indeed, I have,' replied the errant patron, 'I have eaten at the Taj, Maurya, Oberoi, Imperial, Hyatt.'

'What did they say to you when you

rinsed your mouth making all these unpleasant sounds?'

'They asked: "You think this is *Kakey da Hotel*?" And threw me out.'

❑

This Khalistani anecdote has been sent to me by Kanwaljit Kaur and Manohar Bhatia. A Khalistan Roadways bus plying between the state's major towns had a Nihang conductor. 'Where to?' he asked a young Sikh passenger before issuing him a ticket. 'Amritsar,' replied the youngster. The Nihang conductor gave him a clout on the head and said, 'It is Sri Amritsarji Sahib.' The youngster quickly corrected himself, 'Yes, of course! One for Sri Amritsarji Sahib.' The next passenger was a Hindu. 'Where to?' asked the Nihang. 'Sri Ludhianaji Sahib,' replied the other timidly. He too was rewarded with a clout on the head. 'Only Ludhiana, no Sri or Sahibji,' admonished the Nihang before issuing him a ticket. The third passenger happended to be a wordly-wise Marwari. When asked for his destination, he replied: 'Nihangji, kindly give me a ticket for Sri Amritsarji Sahib; thereafter I will go on foot to my village.' The Nihang was pleased: 'If you are not completing your journey by this bus, no need for a ticket-shiket,' he replied.

❒

Deccani Hindustani is a constant source of amusement for northerners. Whenever

I happen to be in the erstwhile domains of His Exalted Highness the Nizam I try to veer the conversation round to make them say *hao* instead of *haan* (yes) or *nakko* instead of *naheen* (no). The words sound sweet when mouthed by young *puttas* (male urchins) or *puttees* (female urchins). The other day I was in Hyderabad's Patthar Gatti bazaar looking for Urdu publications. The going was very *halloo halloo* (slow) because of the chaotic tangle of cycles, cars, tongas and flocks of black-burqa ladies going to Laad Bazar to buy lac-n-glass bangles. I stopped beside a *dargah* beneath the Char Minar where a fellow was lustily blowing through his shehnai hoping to drown out other noises of the city. I heard a lot of *hao*'s and *nakko*'s and asked my escort for an explanation. He told me an anecdote about a Lucknavi gentleman who on a visit to

Hyderabad had like me wanted to know the reason. A highly literate Hyderabadi friend replied: '*Janaab-i-wala*, educated Andhras always say *Jee Haan* for yes sir, it is only the illiterate who say *hao*.'

'You always say *Jee haan*, you must be highly educated.'

'*Hao*.'

❐

An anti-Establishment joke: A vagrant, finding no place on the pavement, parked himself at the feet of a statue of Mahatma Gandhi. At midnight he was woken up by someone gently tapping him with his stick. It was the Mahatma himself. 'You Indians have been unfair to me,' complained the benign spirit. 'You put my statues everywhere that show me either standing or walking. My feet are very tired. Why can't I have a horse like the one Shivaji has? Surely, I did as much for the nation as he! And you still call me your Bapu.'

Next morning the vagrant went round calling on the ministers. At long last he persuaded one to join him for a night-long vigil at the feet of the Mahatma's statue. Lo and behold, as the neighbouring police station gong struck the midnight hour, the Mahatma emerged from his statue to converse with the vagrant. He repeated his complaint of having to stand or walk and his request to be provided a mount like the Chhatrapati's.

'Bapu,' replied the vagrant, 'I am too poor to buy you a horse, but I have brought this minister from the Government for you. He . . .'

Bapu looked at the minister and

remarked: 'I asked for a horse, not a donkey.'

□

Shri O.S. Bhatnagar from Mathura sent us a portion left out of the complaint made by a hapless passenger, whose ablutions resulted in his missing his train.

'While me fall down in hurry to ride the going train I was saw the dam guard shouting the whisle and moving the flag (which contry it was I didn't now), but he keep standing on the platefarum not try enter to the compartment. Was he go by aeroplan to next stashun?

'Make a juge inquiry and sent the results to bearded Happy Time Lion in his den at Horn Bye Road, Mumbai, who passed to me.'

One must not be too hard on a poor fellow whose knowledge of a foreign language is elementary. Much funnier are linguistic *faux pas* committed by those who assume familiarity with a lingo without really knowing it. I recall an angry letter written by a teacher of English to the chairman of her school. 'Dear Sir, I wish to resignate . . .' The sound of words often causes confusion in simple minds. A semi-literate but rich businessman intending to make a bequest to a co-educational institution was dissuaded from doing so by one who wanted the money for his own boys' school. 'Do you know that in the co-ed school boys and girls share the same curriculum?' he asked the donor. 'Moreover, they matriculate together.' To drive the point home, he added: 'And worse than that they spend most of their time in seminars.'

The bequest was never made.

◻

My short piece on Indian mispronunciation of English evoked many examples from our readers. One from the South is indignant that I should have lampooned the Tamilian accent because: 'The very best English is spoken in Tamil Nadu. And the worst by the Punjabis.' Professor Viswanathan from Mangalore writes about his English teacher's advice that the '*Jorality* of the composition lies in the *dadabudality* in the usage of words.' (For the life of me I cannot work out what the learned teacher was trying to say!) He also wrote to say that a Sikh doctor diagnosed some ailment as '*penewmonia*'. That sounds like a very sick Sikh joke!

❐

Winston Churchill, when asked for permission to allow sixty MPs to go up on a trial flight of a newly-designed aircraft, said a firm no. 'I think it would be disastrous if suddenly the country were plunged into sixty by-elections. Besides which, throughout my long public career I have always maintained that it is unwise to put all your *baskets* into one egg.'

❐

Correspondent N. Sharna from Ramgarh (Bihar) sends a clipping of a tender for supply of school equipment put out—of all people—by the office of the District Superintendent of Education. It invited 'Quotationers' to make offers for the following articles:

1. Bras and Bell—1 kg with wooden humber

2. Jumetry set in wooden box

3. Glob—8" dymiter

4. Bucket (Balti) 10"

5. Spad Nos of tata

6. Aluminium mfg for one later

7. Wooden Black Board 1 big 5" x 3½" for shakhua wood with two kari

8. Wooden Black Board (Small) 31½" x 2½" for shakhua wood with two kari

9. Maps: India world Tirhut Commissionary and West Charaparan Rajnaitik and Historical map of Bihar

historical approved by survey department.

10. Charts: Digesting system skelton Health sanitation historical Bhawan Kala Darshan Shambi-dhan Jiwa Vigyan Bhawtik Vigyan Rashayan Vigyan.

Now you know why Biharis are amongst the most illiterate in India.

❏

Robert Atkins, MP had this dig at Khrushchev. At a public meeting the Soviet leader was denouncing Stalin. Somebody from the audience shouted: 'As one of his colleagues at the time, why didn't you stop him?'

There was deathly stillness. Khrushchev thundered, 'Who said that?' There was no response. After a long and petrified silence Khrushchev replied to his question himself, 'Now you know why.'

❏

Epitaph-collecting is my favourite hobby. I have quite a few witty farewells to life in my repertoire. *Two Monsoons* by Theon Wilkinson, who indulged in the same ghoulish pastime, has added two gems to my collection. A soldier drowned in the Chenab has this on his tombstone: 'Out of the depths have I cried unto Thee, O Lord'. Another one in Peshawar runs: 'Here lies Captain Ernest Bloomfield, accidentally shot by his orderly, March 2nd, 1879. Well done, thou good and faithful servant.'

❏

There was the boss of a firm in Australia where absenteeism was endemic. He spoke to the workmen: 'Looking about me I see a number of faces that are not here; what I have to say applies particularly to those who are absent, and I hope they will listen attentively and make a note of every word.'

A similar story is about a signpost at a road junction. 'This way to Timbuktu—if you can't read, enquire at blacksmith's opposite.'

Some signs have a macabre sense of humour as one leading to a cemetery: 'One-way traffic'. An exhortation to city dwellers when they come to seek peace and quiet in the mountains: 'Keep still and listen to the silence'. A number of Aussies follow the instruction and one asks: 'I cannot hear anything, can you?'

❐

Vice-Admiral Lord Mountgarret was addressing an all-male gathering of sailors where everyone present knew as much about sailing as he. His Lordship who had by then imbibed more than his share of spirits decided to talk about his sexual exploits of which he claimed to have had many more than they. The next morning while His Lordship was nursing his hangover in bed, Her Ladyship ran into a member of the previous evening's audience while she was out shopping and asked him how her husband's speech had gone down. 'He was a roaring success,' the man assured her.

'I am so glad,' said Lady Mountgarret. 'I was terribly worried. He's only done it three times, you see. The first time he was violently sick. The second time his hat blew off, and the third time he got all tangled up in the sheets!'

It is a great pity that our legislators lose their tempers so readily. Much more can be achieved by ready wit than by angry demonstration, yelling slogans, abuse, fisticuffs or walk-outs. I recall an encounter between the late Feroze Gandhi and a senior cabinet minister, given to acid remarks about everyone and with an exaggerated notion of his own ability. This minister was said to have described Feroze Gandhi as the 'Prime Minister's lap-dog'. Then he had the misfortune of getting involved in a financial scandal. Feroze Gandhi was scheduled to open the debate in the Lok Sabha. He is said to have walked up to the minister and within the hearing of the Treasury benches said: 'Mr So-and-So, I hear you have been describing me as a lap-dog. You no doubt consider yourself a pillar of the state. Today I will do to you what a dog usually does to a pillar.'

Once I gave an example of a repartee in the Lok Sabha. I have just stumbled on a perfect gem—of all places from what must be one of the smallest democracies in the world, Uruguay. An angry senator was attacking a minister of government. The minister tried to interrupt the senator's speech. 'I haven't finished yet,' roared the senator, and went on in his near-defamatory tirade. Each time the minister tried to protest, the Senator yelled, 'I haven't finished yet.' At long last when the speech ended, the minister asked, 'Have you finished now?'

'Yes,' replied the senator, taking his seat.

'Then pull the chain.'

❏

Two IRA men were driving to the location where they intended to plant a time-bomb which one of them had in his lap. 'Drive a little slower—this bomb may go off any minute,' said the man carrying the explosive. 'Don't worry,' assured the driver, 'we've got a spare one in the boot.'

❑

I owe this follow-up on the making of a minister to Dr I.C. Dawoodbhoy of Mumbai.

'The son was expected from abroad after a five-year jaunt. The father invited his best friend to his house on the day of arrival and took him to a room where the son was to be shown in. He pointed to the four things he had placed on the table. 'If he picks up the money,' he said, 'he will be a businessman. If he takes the Bible, he will be a pious, religious man. If the bottle of liquor, he will be a drunkard and a waster. And if he picks up the gun, he is going to be a gangster.' Both of them waited behind the curtain and watched. As the son walked in he noticed the four items on the table. He opened the bottle of whisky and took a long swig; he pocketed the wad of currency notes, put the gun in his hip pocket and the Bible under his arm and calmly walked away. 'Dammit,' said the father, 'he is going to be a minister.'

❐

Once every three months or so an elderly lady who was once prominent in the women's movement calls on me. She brushes aside my secretary, ignores the notice saying, 'No visitors before 11 a.m. and thereafter only by appointment,' opens the door and asks, 'Can I see you for a moment?' and without waiting for an answer enters the room. She is well-meaning and soft-spoken. I offer her a chair. She takes time to compose herself by covering her face with her hands and thinking deep thoughts. Then she bares her smiling face and starts the dialogue with the question: 'Sardar sahib, tell me, where is our country going to?'

I shrug my shoulders and make some helpless noises which imply, 'I don't know.' She is satisfied and puts her second question: 'What are you doing about it?' I hold up my hands in a gesture of helpless resignation and reply: 'What can I do?' She tells me what a pleasure it is to discuss national problems with someone as well informed as me and takes her leave.

❏

Lady Reading seldom lost her Viceregal poise and attended every function in spite of failing health. Sir Conrad Corfield, an ICS officer in India for twenty-two years, relates the following incident in his book, *The Princely India I Knew*. One evening, when the Viceroy's orchestra was performing during dinner, she enquired about the title of the dance tune which was being played. No one could remember. So her ADC was sent to ask the bandmaster.

The conversation at the table changed to another subject during the ADC's

absence. He slipped into his seat on return and waited for an opportunity to impart his information. At the next silence he leant forward to catch Lady Reading's eye and, in a penetrating voice, said, 'I will remember your kisses, Your Excellency, when you have forgotten my name.'

❑

A wealthy Maheshwari, the richest of the Marwari community, was complaining about his wife's spendthrift habits to a friend. 'One day she asked me for ten rupees, the next day she asked me for twenty and this morning she wanted twenty-five. She is the limit.'

'She certainly is,' agreed the friend. 'What did she do with all that money?'

'*Main kya jaanoon*' (how should I know), replied the wealthy man. 'I never gave her any.'

☐

A firm which undertakes to destroy vermin has sent me its terms of contract. If its ability to kill pests is as great as its ability to kill the English *bhasha* then I can strongly commend it. Instructions are:

1. Before start the work empted every thing.

2. In the bed room cuboards to be empted.

3. When the Job is started, nobody can stay inside after fumigation to keep two hours in the Flat.

4. After open the Flat only clean with dry cloth.

Nurul Alam from Silchar sends me a few lovely samples of bureaucratic wit of the days of the British Raj. One is an entry made by an executive engineer in the visitors' book of a Circuit House:

'The veranda of the Circuit House badly needs railings. During my momentary absence, a cow ate up some estimates which I had left lying on a table in the veranda.' Below this note was the commissioner's observation: 'I find it hard to believe that even cows could swallow PWD estimates.'

In another Circuit House book another executive engineer had noted: 'The washbasin should be immediately replaced. I could not wash my face properly for want of proper facilities.' Against this entry is a marginal note in the commissioner's beautiful hand: 'SDO will replace the washbasin at once. The executive engineer had to wash his face in tears during his last visit to this station.'

The prize remark is against a complaint that the latrine was too far away from the bungalow. 'He should have started earlier,' wrote the wit.

❏

I have so many amusing anecdotes on Prem Kirpal, his love of good food and wine (he drank more liquor off me than off himself), his vast collection of unread books, his absentmindedness etc. However I'll break my vow and tell you one about his habit of talking loudly over the phone. We were sitting in the crowded lobby of a hotel in Madrid when he was summoned to the telephone booth in a corner of the hall. Without shutting the door Kirpal began to yell into the phone: 'Lizbeth! Hello! How are you?' People in the lobby stopped talking. Everyone was amused. He came back and announced to me, 'That was Elizabeth Adiseshiah, you know?'

'Yes,' I replied sarcastically, 'so does everyone else in the lobby.'

'Was I talking very loudly? Her hotel is five miles away, you know!'

It reminded me of Winston Churchill's retort to a minister who shared the next cubicle and was wont to talk at the top of his voice. He sent his secretary to tell the minister to lower his voice. The secretary came back and explained, 'Sir, Mr Brown is talking to Scotland.'

'I know,' replied Winston Churchill, 'tell him to use the telephone.'

❏

I recall an incident during one of the general elections when an unusually self-righteous and aggressive Janata candidate confronted a staunch Congressman. 'After all the evil deeds done by the Congress party during the Emergency how can you vote for that party?' he asked. Unabashed the Congressman replied: 'I am a Congressman because my father and before him his father were for the Congress.'

'Aha!' exclaimed the Janata candidate triumphantly, hoping to squash the voter. 'If your father was a donkey and before him his father also a donkey, what would that make you?'

'That, Sir,' retorted the voter, 'would make me Janata.'

Here are two similar linguistic lapses committed by men expected to have better acquaintance with English. One was the late Radha Raman, once a mighty pillar of the Delhi administration. At a buffet dinner the Prime Minister pressed him to help himself to some food. 'Not yet,' replied Raman, 'I'll eat only after the Prime Minister passed away.'

Once I was hosting a lunch for a minister. When I offered the dessert to him, he wagged his head and said: 'No, thank you! I am quite fed up.'

Vasant Sathe, intending to compliment Sharada Prasad, author of the text, and Satyan for the photographs, in the lavishly produced book on Karnataka remarked: 'You two have immoralized Karnataka!' Vasant certainly immortalized himself.

My favourite story of a linguistic *faux pas* is of a friend who broke wind somewhat loudly in mixed company. Overcome with embarrassment he stuttered: 'Sorry, it was a slip of the tongue.'

❐

Once upon a time there was a nonconformist swallow who decided not to fly south for the winter. However, when the weather turned very cold, it reluctantly started to fly southwards. In a short time ice began to form on its wings and it fell to earth in a barnyard frozen still. A cow passed by and crapped on the little swallow. The swallow thought it was the end. But the dung warmed it and defrosted its wings. Warm and happy, able to breathe, it started to chirp. Just then a large tomcat came by and hearing the chirping, found out where it was coming from, clawed away the dung and devoured the swallow.

Moral: Everyone who shits on you is not necessarily your enemy; everyone who gets you out of the shit is not necessarily your friend; and if you're warm and happy in a pile of shit, keep your mouth shut.

◻

This exchange took place many years ago between the then finance minister John Mathai and Acharya Kripalani. The Acharya is renowned for his acid tongue. He was going for the civil service and injected a particularly waspish anecdote about a young man who having knocked at many doors to find a job returned crestfallen to his father. The father reassured him: 'I know you are a no-good son of a gun. No one in his senses will employ you. But don't lose hope, you can always get a government job; they are meant for worthless people like you.'

John Mathai was quick to reply: 'Having heard the Acharya's observation with great respect, I am coming to the conclusion that Acharyaji is fast becoming ripe for a government job.'

❐

This story, which appeared in the *Times* (London) highlights the humiliations the civil servants have to suffer at the hands of ministers. There was this civil servant who retired after forty years of slogging in his office. He rented a small cottage near a village and went into a self-imposed *vanprastha*. The villagers became very curious about him. But all they saw was that every morning a boy came to his door, rang the bell and spoke a sentence. The civil servant replied with a sentence and handed him a coin. When curiosity got the better of the village folk, they approached the boy and asked him what passed between them. 'Nothing much,' replied the lad, 'he's hired me to ring his bell and say to him "Sir, the minister wants to see you!" And he replies: "Tell the bloody minister to bugger off." For this he pays me ten pence a day.'

A Nihang decided to stop an express

train at a non-stop station. He stood in the middle of the track brandishing his *kirpan* and yelling defiance at the oncoming train. A crowd watched the confrontation with bated breath. When the engine driver noticed the Nihang on the track and realized he would not be able to stop the train in time, he blew his whistle as frantically as he could. Just as the engine was almost upon him, the Nihang jumped aside and let the train pass.

'What happened Nihangji?' asked the onlookers. 'Did you take fright?'

'Never!' replied the Nihang with bravado. 'You see how I made it scream? A Nihang never kills anyone who cries for mercy.'

❐

Sindhis are known both for their sharp practices as well as for their clanishness: they drive hard bargains but also help fellow Sindhis to find employment. The following story was told to me by a Sindhi businessman on a visit to Hong Kong. He wanted to have a silk suit made and went to a Sindhi tailor's shop at the airport which advertised suits made to measure in a couple of hours. The visiting businessman selected the material and asked how much it cost. The tailor replied: 'Sir, seeing you are a fellow Sindhi I will offer you a special price. A suit of this material costs 200 Hong Kong dollars—as you can see clearly marked on the label. I charge everyone else two hundred dollars but not a fellow Sindhi. I won't ask for 190 dollars, not even 180 dollars. For you it will be 170 dollars, not a cent more.'

'Why should you lose money on me

just because I happen to be a fellow Sindhi?' replied the visitor. 'So what should I offer for this suit? Seventy dollars? That I would to a non-Sindhi tailor. Eighty dollars? That would be insulting a Sindhi brother. I offer you ninety. dollars and not a cent less.'

'Okay. That's a deal,' replied the tailor.

❐

In a crowded railway compartment one berth was occupied by a man covered from head to foot with his bedsheet. A porter entered and without much ado proceeded to belabour the recumbent figure with blows and abuse: *O! Jagtara, teri maan di. O! Jagtara, teri bhain di . . .* etc. etc. After a while the other passengers intervened, uncovered the recumbent man's face and asked him why he was taking all the fisticuffs and abuse without a protest.

'The joke is on this fellow,' he replied. 'He'll soon tire of beating me—and in any case I am not Jagtara.'

❐

An essay on *Geese* submitted by a schoolboy reads:

'Geese is a low heavy-set bird which is mostly meat and feathers. His head is one side and he sits on the other. Geese can't sing much on account of the dampness of the moisture. He's got no between the toes and he's got a little balloon in his stomach to keep him from sinking.

'Some geese, when they get big, has curls on their tails and is called ganders. Ganders don't have it and hatch but just sit and loaf and go swimming. If I was goose, I would rather be a gander.'

❏

A young Punjabi couple who I hardly knew insisted that I come to their house-warming party. I went suitably armed with compliments for the hostess and her new home. They had obviously spent a lot of money—a long drive-in flanked by royal palms and beds of roses led up to the portico. There was apparently an even larger spread of lawns and flowerbeds in the rear of the house. I fired my first compliment at the house.

'What a beautiful frontage you have, Mrs Kumar!'

'Oh, thank you, thank you,' she gushed, 'but you have not seen my backside yet. It's much prettier than my front.'

My second compliment evoked an equally naïve response. She was draped in a gossamer-thin sari through which one could see most of what she had. 'And what a beautiful sari you are wearing!' I said.

'Oh this is very *maamooli*. I just wear it for streetwalking.'

❏

A young reader sends a South Indian version of how to spell Mississippi. 'First comes yumm. Then I come. Then sissi. Then peepee. Then I come again.'

A busload of American tourists were heading towards Punjab on G.T. Road when suddenly the driver slammed on the brakes.

Lying on the road in front was a Sardarji with his ear to the ground. Passengers trooped out of the bus and crowded around the man. 'Hey, what are you doing down there pal?' asked one of the tourists.

The man slowly raised his head and replied: 'Green Matador 25 km away travelling at 80 km.'

'Wow,' exclaimed the tourist, 'you can tell us that by listening to the road?'

'No,' croaked the Sardarji, 'I fell off the damned thing.'

❐

A group of Congress (I) MPs were comparing notes with one another during the Rajiv Gandhi era. As usual their chief occupation was who was *nazdeek* (close) to the Prime Minister and who had been replaced by whom in the inner circles. Asked one of another who seemed to know the comings and goings on Race Course Road: 'Have you seen the Prime Minister recently?'

'*Arre kahan!* You ring and ring and no appointment is given. "Too busy" is all that his secretaries say.'

'But surely, you know him well enough to walk into the *kothi* without an appointment.'

'Those days are gone,' replied the other sadly, 'now it's battalions outside and Italians inside.'

Two Punjabi farmers ploughing their fields saw a Mig-23 fly overhead at great speed, emitting a lot of smoke from its tail. One remarked, 'Bantia, look how fast it is going and the racket it is making!'

'Sure', replied the other, 'if somebody set fire to your tail, you would run faster than the plane and fart much louder.'

❐

A minister of government, whose knowledge of English was very poor, was provided with a secretary to write speeches for him. 'Give me a fifteen-minute speech on the non-aligned movement,' ordered the boss.

The text was prepared to last exactly fifteen minutes. But when the minister proceeded to make his oration it took him half-an-hour to do so. The organizers of the conference were upset because their schedule went haywire. And the minister was upset because his secretary had let him down. He upbraided him: 'I asked for a fifteen-minute speech; you gave me a half-hour speech. Why?' he demanded.

'Sir, I gave a fifteen-minute speech. But you read out its carbon copy as well.'

❑

This one I picked up in London on my way back home. As the aircraft was taxiing towards the runway to take off, the voice on the speaker welcomed passengers on board and introduced them to the pilot. 'Your captain is Miss Mary Joystick . . .'

'You mean to tell me this plane is being piloted by a woman?' asked an alarmed passenger to a stewardess.

'Yes, sir,' replied the stewardess. 'So is the co-pilot, Miss Jane Understudy. So also are the radio operator and the navigator, they are all women in command.'

'I must see this for myself,' said the passenger. 'Please take me to the cockpit.'

'We don't call it that any more, sir,' replied the stewardess.

❐

Regarding the benefits of abstinence, you may have heard the repartee between the abstainer General Montogomery and the gay liver, Winston Churchill. Says Monty: 'I don't drink, I don't smoke and

I am 100 per cent fit.' Answers Winnie: 'I smoke, I drink and I am 200 per cent fit.'

My favourite is the one about an ageing rogue who wanted to live to be a hundred. 'Give up smoking, drinking and going out with women,' advised his doctor.

'And will I then be able to live up to one hundred years?' asked the rogue.

'I am not sure,' replied the doctor, 'but it will certainly seem like it.'

❑

I never object to anyone calling me names or making fun of me. I believe in Burn's dictum to 'see ourselves as others see us'. Many of my readers see me as a name-dropper and a poseur. P.S. Ranganathan of New Delhi has parodied what he thinks I would have written on the deaths of Tagore, Marilyn Monroe and Karl Marx. The obit on the poet reads as follows:

'It was a rainy Sunday morning when I had the opportunity to meet the Nobel Prize winner. Tagore was at a seaside resort in Switzerland, the charming landlocked country of Europe. I was just returning after a two-month holiday-cum-research tour of Polynesia, Hawaii and Las Vegas. I was working on a novel for my publishers, Tom, Dick and Harry, London. This novel was also to be published in America by Fung, Wag and Kneel Inc, New York.

'I had earlier phoned Tagore for an appointment. "Sunday, 7.30. Will it suit you?" he asked in a clear voice. "Oh, anything will suit me except my suits stitched in India," I said. There was hearty laughter at the other end of the phone.

Surely, Tagore was a man with a high sense of humour!

'When I went on the appointed day, I was slightly late—to be exact, by about eight hours. Tagore received me at the porch and offered me *nimbu de joiuce*, a delicious drink (certainly, I did not expect the poet to offer me Scotch). For the next forty minutes we discussed the current literary trends. I was then vaguely planning a novel, later to be titled *Train to Pakistan* (published by Hind Pocket Books or Orient Paperbacks or Pearl Publications. I don't exactly remember the name of the publisher, which is not quite material. The book is priced at Rs 4, which is quite material).

'Tagore asked me what I was doing. "Nothing of importance," I said. "Oh, you Sardarjis are modest to a fault. With your remarkable talent, whatever you do will be important and will certainly make a great impact on the minds of intellectuals. Now, since we are alone, I can tell you this. Your writings are quite outstanding and you are sure to be awarded the Nobel Prize.'

'Tagore was a great soul with a great heart. He is gone. I only wish that his statement comes true.'

About Miss Monroe, the parody reads as follows: 'Marilyn had a soft corner for me. It was just by chance that I was seated next to her in a Pan Am jet from New York to London. "Mr Khushwant, I presume, I am Marilyn Monroe," she introduced herself. "Your name is familiar. But I am unable to place you," I said hesitatingly. "You must have seen a naked picture of a Hollywood actress in *Life*. It was mine," she said. Then I remembered.'

And Karl Marx:

'An outstanding thinker and a remarkable writer who was fascinated by my writings. In fact he told a common friend of ours—why should I withhold his name, he was Winston Churchill—well, Marx was telling Winston that he was keen to translate my novel into Russian. Winny—that was how I used to address him—later told me this when we met at Buckingham Palace for a party. I was thrilled by this piece of news but had to politely decline the offer since another friend of mine was already on the job. If my readers would not say I am dropping names, I can say that the friend was no other person than Tolstoy. This is what one "K" can write about another "K" in this moment of great anguish.'

If this be the truth about me, it is time for me to take an overdose of barbiturates.

One day Gorbachev, Reagan and Rajiv Gandhi appeared before God to find out what was in store for their countries. Gorbachev asked: 'When will my country be free from corruption?'

'Twenty-six years from now,' replied God.

Reagan put the same question to him. God replied: 'It'll take time. At least another century.'

'What about India?' asked Rajiv Gandhi.

God had tears in His eyes as He replied, 'I won't live to see the day when India will be free of corruption.'

❏

An argument arose as to which state

government excelled in corruption. The following story settled the issue.

Six years ago an MLA from Kerala visited Chandigarh and called on a Punjab minister at his house. He was amazed at the ostentation and asked his old friend, 'How did you manage to acquire so much wealth?'

'Are you really interested in knowing?'

'Of course, yes. A little extra knowledge always helps.'

'Then wait till tomorrow, and I shall explain fully.'

The next day the minister drove the MLA down the highway for several kilometres in his personal Honda.

He stopped the car, both of them got out and the minister pointed his finger to a spot down the beautiful valley.

'Do you see the big bridge over there?' he asked.

'Yes,' replied the MLA.

'Half the cost of the bridge went into my pocket.'

Four years later the Punjabi who in the meantime lost his portfolio, went on a holiday to Trivandrum and called on his old friend, who in the meanwhile had become a minister. 'By God,' said the Punjabi, 'you have beaten me flat. Crystal chandeliers, Italian marble, Mercedes. Tell me how you managed it.'

'I will tell you tomorrow,' said the minister.

Next day the minister drove him down the highway, stopped the car at a spot overlooking a valley and pointed his finger to a spot down the valley, asking, 'Do you see the bridge over there?'

'I see no bridge,' said the Punjabi.

'Quite right,' said the minister. 'The entire cost of the bridge went into my pocket.'

A Punjabi peasant on his first flight to take up a job in England got a seat on a British airline. Came lunch time and the stewardess brought a tray of European savouries. 'No,' said the peasant firmly as he undid a small bundle and took out a *makki ki roti*. 'What is this you are munching?' asked the stewardess.

'This bread India,' he replied.

A little while later, the stewardess brought a trayful of puddings of different kinds. Once again the peasant shook his head as he produced a lump of gur from his pocket and put it in his mouth.

'What is this you are chewing?' asked the stewardess.

'This sweet India,' he replied.

When the stewardess came to take away the lunch trays, the peasant let out a loud belch.

'And what is this?' demanded the

stewardess sternly.

'This is air India.'

□

Rajiv Gandhi, Hinduja and Amitabh decided to become partners and make a film. Hinduja said: 'I will put up the money for the film!'

Amitabh said: 'I will act in the film!'

Both of them then turned to Rajiv and asked: 'What will you do for the film?'

Rajiv said: '*Hum dekhenge . . .*' (I shall see).

□

The harried clerk suffering from

insomnia never got to sleep before dawn; then slept right through the alarm and so never made it to the office on time. Upon being reprimanded by his boss, he decided to consult a doctor. The doctor gave him some sleeping pills. That night he fell asleep immediately and had a pleasant rest. In the morning he awoke before the alarm rang, jumped out of the bed with new verve and vigour. When he arrived at his office promptly, he told his boss, 'Those pills I got from my doctor really work. I had no trouble at all waking up this morning.'

'That's nice,' the boss replied, 'but where were you yesterday?'

❏

We Indians are often called a litigious lot and many of us despair on the practice of our labyrinthine legal system. But perhaps many of us are not aware that American lawyers are no less mercenary than their Indian counterparts and some of the legal judgments handed down by US courts will amaze us.

For example, in 1984, an American woman under the influence of drink drove her Porsche 60 mph in a 25 mph zone and killed a man. Result? Porsche was asked by a US court to pay $2.5 million in damages for having designed a car deemed too high in performance for an average driver.

Another example: while attempting to burgle a school a burglar fell through the skylight. The company that insured the school was asked to pay $250,000 in damages and give the would-be burglar $1500 per month for life.

The joke goes that Americans can be divided into three broad groups and each group deals with its enemies in its own way. Americans belonging to the first group sue their enemy. Those belonging to the second group shoot their enemy. And those belonging to the third group shoot their enemy and then sue his widow for mental anguish brought about by guilt and imprisonment!

❑

A car was involved in an accident in a street. As expected a large crowd gathered. A newspaper reporter anxious to get his story could not get near the car. But being a bright young fellow, he started crying loudly, 'Let me through! Let me through!

I am the son of the victim.'

The crowd made way for him. Lying in front of the damaged car was the donkey it had run over.

❑

'I understand you had an argument with your wife?'

'Yes.'

'How did it end?'

'Ultimately she came down on her knees—and said, "If you are a man, come out from beneath the bed and fight like a man!" '

❑

Seen inside a DTC bus:

Aana free

Jaana free

Pakray gaye to

Khana free

(You can get in for free

You can get out for free

If you happen to get caught

You'll get dinner for free)

☐

The home minister sent a registered letter to the Akali leaders ensconced in the Yatri Niwas of the Golden Temple: 'Hand over the culprit at once', it demanded.

Promptly came the reply from Jarnail Singh Bhindranwale: 'We have a Harpreet

Singh and Gurpreet Singh and a Jaspreet
Singh but we have no Kulpreet Singh.'

❐

A   judge, irritated by a lawyer's
behaviour, admonished him, 'You are
crossing the limits.'

'*Kaun saala aisa kehta hai*,' roared the
lawyer.

'How dare you call me *saala*—brother-
in-law? I'll have you charged for contempt
of court,' said the judge angrily.

'My Lord misunderstood me,' replied
the lawyer coolly, 'I do not call you *saala*,
all I said was *kaun sa* law *aisa kahta hai*—
which law says so?'

❐

Three friends, a Hindu, a Muslim and a Sikh, were discussing intimate matrimonial problems. How best to send a signal to the wife that the husband desired her company?

'I have evolved a formula,' said Rehman. 'All I have to say is, "Begum, you are looking like a newly-wed bride"— and she knows what I have on my mind.'

'I have a similar formula,' said Sham Lal. 'I ask her if she is wearing the same sari she wore on the wedding night. She gets the signal.'

'Why this *gol mol*, roundabout approach?' questioned Banta Singh. 'When I want her company, I simply ring the bell and she comes over to my room.'

'This is wonderful,' agreed his friends. 'But how does she communicate to you that she wants your company?'

'She has her own formula,' replied

Banta Singh. 'She asks me, "Sardarji, *tuseen ghantee tay naheen vajaaee?*" Sardarji, did you ring for me?'

□

A young entrant to the army was posted at a non-family station for many years. When he got news of a son born to his wife he had left behind in the village, he entertained his pals and told them that he had decided to name his son Pandey. 'Why?' asked his friends.

'In our village the neighbours are very co-operative,' he explained, 'and so we number our children according to their vicinity. If it is neighbour number two, we name the child Dua; if it is number three, he is named Trivedi; number four

Chaturvedi. In my case, it was neighbour number five, so he is named Pandey.'

His friends were nonplussed. 'What if it is the produce of a mixture of neighbours?'

'Then we call him Mishri.'

'Disgusting!' they remarked. 'What if the paternity is unknown?'

'That's very simple, we name him Gupta.'

'What happens if the mother is too shy to divulge the identity of the father?'

'Then we name him Sharma.'

❏

Two Hindi speaking friends who were trying hard to learn English decided to correspond with each other in *angrezee*.

The first letter went somewhat as follows:
'My dear *mitr*, I am in the well. I hope you
are also in the well.'

❐

The following ad appeared in a daily
paper: 'Are you illiterate? You don't know
how to read or write? If so, do write to us
and let us help you.'

❐

Anne Landers's syndicated column is
not famous for wit or humour; it is largely
devoted to 'Dear Diary' kind of confessions
and emotional yearnings. But this piece
sent to me by Inder Gujral is truly hilarious.

I reproduce it in totality, in ignorance of copyright. In any event it is not by Anne Landers but by one of her many readers who sent it to her. It is about problems that can arise if you give a dog a bad name. This is how it goes:

'Everybody who has a dog calls him "Rover" or "Boy". I call mine "Sex". He's a great pal but he has caused me a great deal of embarrassment.

'When I went to city hall to renew his dog licence, I told the clerk I would like a licence for Sex. He said, "I'd like one, too!" Then I said: "But this is a dog." He said he didn't care what she looked like. Then I said, "You don't understand, I've had Sex since I was nine years old." He winked and said, "You must have been quite a kid."

'When I got married and went on my honeymoon, I took the dog with me. I told the motel clerk that I wanted a room for my wife and me and a special room for Sex.

'He said: "You don't need a special room. As long as you pay your bill we don't care what you do." I said: "Look, you don't seem to understand, Sex keeps me awake at night." The clerk said: "Funny, I have the same problem."

'One day I entered Sex in a contest, but before the competition began, the dog ran away. Another contestant asked me why I was just standing there, looking disappointed. I told him I had planned to have Sex in the contest. He told me I should have sold my own tickets. "But you don't understand," I said, "I had hoped to have Sex on TV." He said: "Now that cable is all over the place, it's no big deal anymore."

'When my wife and I separated, we

went to court to fight for custody of the dog. I said: "Your Honour, I had Sex before I was married." The judge said: "The courtroom isn't a confessional. Stick to the case, please."

'Then I told him that after I was married, Sex left me. He said: "Me, too."

'Last night Sex ran off again. I spent hours looking around town for him. A cop came over to me and asked, "What are you doing in this alley at four o'clock in the morning?" I told him that I was looking for Sex. My case comes up on Friday.'

❏

A Panditji and a Maulvi sahib happened to be close neighbours in some posh locality of Delhi. Even though both were good friends, there was a certain amount of competition between them. If one had his drive done up, the other had his relaid and so it went on.

One day the Panditji had a new custom-built Chevrolet, so the Maulana bought a Mercedes. When the Maulana looked out of his window it was to see the Panditji pouring water over the top of the car bonnet. He opened the window and shouted, 'That's not the way to fill the radiator, you know.'

'Aha,' said the Panditji, 'I am purifying it with Ganga jal, that's more than you can do to yours.'

A little while later, the Panditji was taken aback to see the Maulvi sahib lying in the middle of road, hack-saw in hand, sawing off the last inch of his car's exhaust pipe.

In his introduction to *Fabulous Oriental Recipes*, Johna Blinn lists the following:

'Happy Home Recipe'

4 cups Love

2 cups Loyalty

5 quarts Faith

2 tablespoons Tenderness

1 cup Kindness

5 cups Understanding

3 cups Forgiveness

1 cup Friendship

5 teaspoons Hope

1 barrel Laughter

Sunshine to taste

Take Love and Loyalty; mix thoroughly with Faith. Blend with Tenderness, Kindness, Understanding and Forgiveness. Add Friendship and Hope; sprinkle abundantly with Laughter. Bake with Sunshine. Serve with generous helpings.

Two pandits riding on a scooter were stopped by a Punjab police constable. 'Don't you know riding pillion is forbidden in Punjab?' asked the constable. 'I am going to challan you.'

The pandits pleaded their innocence of rules but he refused to let them go. Very exasperated, the pandit who was driving the scooter replied, 'All right, *Ishwar* is with us. Do what you like.'

'In that case, I'll challan you for having two on the pillion behind you.'

❐

This is about the spelling of the word 'assassination'. A boy who was having trouble remembering the sequence of letters was provided with the following formula: An ass after another, after that I, followed by nation.

☐

A joke doing the rounds of Delhi's diplomatic cocktail circuit, though slightly over the line of propriety, deserves to be told because it illustrates the kind of feelings that obtain between Indians and Pakistanis. It is said that the President of the Soviet Union was celebrating his silver jubilee. As head of state he desired that all countries accredited by it should present him with the best of their products. First came the American ambassador with a brand new Cadillac. The President graciously accepted the gift. It was followed by the British ambassador presenting the latest model of a Rolls Royce. The President was delighted and desired that his thanks be conveyed to Queen Elizabeth II. The next was the ambassador of Israel. He had brought a new variety of elongated lemon developed in his country. The President was furious and ordered the lemon to be put up the Israeli's posterior. Then came the Indian ambassador. He presented a luscious Alphonso mango. The President was not amused and ordered the fruit to be stuffed up the Indian's behind. Having been subjected to the painful insult the Israeli and the Indian ambassadors met in the lobby of the Kremlin Palace. The Israeli looked woebegone. The Indian was wreathed in smiles.

The Israeli asked the Indian, 'How can you manage to look so happy after what has been done to you?'

The Indian ambassador replied, 'You've no idea what is in store for the ambassador of Pakistan. He has brought the largest watermelon developed in his country.'

❏

Hitler and Mussolini go to hell after their death. There they meet God. God asks them to come to his room one at a time. The first call is for Hitler. He goes inside. God asks him, 'Hitler, how many women have you had . . .' He replies, 'Sir, one and only one.'

God says, 'Very good,' gifts him a Mercedes and tells him to have a nice time.

Now it's Mussolini's turn. He goes

inside and is asked the same question. He replies, 'Sir, six.' God gets very annoyed and tells him, 'Take this Ambassador.'

After some time when Mussolini is taking a ride in his car, he hears Hitler laughing very loudly. He gets very angry, gets out of the car and asks Hitler, 'Why are you laughing at me?' He replies, 'Mussolini, I am not laughing at you. Just now I saw the Pope whiz past on skates!'

❐

A youngster rushed into a barber's shop and asked to be given a haircut and a shave immediately. 'You wait your turn young man,' said the barber, 'I will get to you after the others waiting before you have been attended to. It will take an hour or two.'

The young fellow ran out of the barber's shop. He came the next day, the day after and for many days subsequently. Every time he was told to wait his turn, he fled. Not being able to contain his curiosity, the barber asked his assistant to follow the young man and find out where he came from and where he went after leaving his shop.

The assistant did so and reported back: 'I don't know where the fellow comes from but as soon as you tell him you will be busy for the next hour or two, he runs to your home.'

❐

A tough Haryanvi peasant swaggered into a restaurant and ordered for an empty tumbler and a lemon. He asked everyone to look as he squeezed the lemon into the glass with his powerful hands. 'If anyone here can get as much out of a lemon as I have I will give him five rupees.'

A thin, bespectacled clerk accepted the challenge. With his frail hands he got more juice out of the lemon than the Haryanvi. 'Wonderful!' exclaimed the Chaudhary, handing over the fiver. 'But tell me how did you manage to squeeze out more than I?'

'I am from the income tax department,' replied the little fellow.

❏

A little boy was asked by his teacher how one should address the Pope.

'Your Sanctity,' he answered.

'And the Queen of England?'

'Your Majesty.'

'Very good! And what about Ayatollah Khomeini of Iran?'

'Your Funda-mentality,' the boy answered.

❏

During the British Raj an English commander of an Army Cantt in Madras joined a dinner hosted by the jawans to celebrate a local festival. The menu was typically Madrasi.

Next morning at breakfast he commented to his wife, 'Today I have discovered why the bloody Indians use water in the lavatory; toilet paper could catch fire.'

A Sardarji was boasting about the number of cities he had been to: London, Paris, New York, Rome, Karachi.

'You must know Geography quite well,' remarked one of his audience.

'Oh very well,' replied the Sardarji, 'I spent four days in Geography.'

❏

Question: Why is a bad government like a bikini?

Answer: Because people marvel at what's holding it up. And they wish it would fall.

❏

A government servant went to a doctor. 'Doctor sahib, I am suffering from exhaustion. Please advise me.'

The doctor examined him carefully before replying, 'What you need is complete rest. You should return to the office as soon as you can.'

❐

B anta Singh, like all good Sardars, always greeted everyone in the congregation with a loud '*Wahey Guruji ki Khalsa, Wahey Guruji ki Fateh*'. After spending a few years in England he returned home and at the village gurudwara produced an Anglicized version of the greeting: 'Sat Sri Akal. And a copy to all.'

❐

My friend Onkar Singh who returned from Ahmedabad last week posed a question which I could not answer. 'How is it that in Gujarat where every man is a *bhai* and every woman a *ben* the population keeps on increasing?'

J.P. Singh Kaka has drawn my attention to the same kind of confusion that exists in the minds of some people. A bachelor on the lookout for a wife was advised by a friend to put in an ad in the matrimonial columns. He took the advice. A few weeks later his friends asked him if he had any luck. 'Yes,' replied the bachelor and added naïvely, '*Kaee bahnon kay to khat bhee aaye hain*—many sisters have written to me.'

❏

My friend Lakhan Naqvi told me of a

dream he had some months ago of my dying and being resurrected. I was so tickled by it as a kind of summary of my life that I thought of sharing it with my readers.

The wire services reported that I was seriously ill. (I doubt if my illness will merit reportage from either PTI or UNI.) The next morning he read that I had proceeded towards my 'heavenly abode'. He decided to call and condole with my family. He saw me laid out in a coffin. As he came to put some flowers on my corpse, I said, 'Lakhan, get me a bottle of Scotch.'

Lakhan was startled and replied, 'You are supposed to be dead. You are not meant to talk after you die.'

I replied, 'Some lazy people go dumb when they die. Active people like me can go on talking till they are cremated. Get me a bottle of Scotch.'

Lakhan, being a good boy, dutifully got a bottle of Scotch and placed it by my side.

I was taken to the crematorium. As the mourners were returning to their homes, Lakhan, who was by then in his car, saw me coming out of the cremation ground. He opened the door of his car to let me in. 'What happened?' he asked somewhat stupefied. 'How did you manage to survive the cremation?'

'I bribed Yama with the bottle of Scotch you gave me. He let me return to the world. Take me back home,' I replied.

❏

Sardarni Banta Singh was talking to her neighbour, Sardarni Santa Singh, across the balcony. '*Bhainjee*, how have you managed to break your hushand's bad habit of coming home late every night?' asked the former.

'Simple,' replied the latter, 'one night when my husband was very late, I shouted, "Is that you Inderjeet . . .?" He never stayed out late after that.'

❑

We are familiar with the witticisms written behind trucks and three-wheelers. Variations on their themes make interesting reading. For instance, there is the common one: 'If you can read this, UR2 close.' Amusing variation can be: 'If you can read this, you are evidently literate. Congrats!'

There is another one often seen on

the roads: 'Don't come close to me. I hardly know you.' We can improve on it: 'Don't come close to me—I have AIDS.'

I have seen this one on a three-wheeler: 'When I grow up, I'm going to become a Rolls Royce.' Having learnt something of the way Delhi's buses are driven, one can improve on it: 'When I grow up, I am going to become a DTC bus.'

For 'My other car is a Mercedez Benz,' we can alter it slightly to read: 'My other car was sold to buy this one.'

We can also convert 'Life begins at forty; so let's really live it up,' to a warning against overspeeding: 'Life begins at forty—fines begin at fifty.'

◘

The following words of wisdom appear in Shri Amrit Lal's astrological column in *Sunday* of 12 February 1989.

'A splendid opportunity will come your way this week . . . Problems may arise on the professional front so much so that you may even lose your job . . .'

❏

This is a true story of a correspondence which went awry because of a typing error. The stenographer working in the physics department of the university applied for one month's leave. The head of the department agreed, and asked him to type out an application to the registrar asking for a substitute. Instead of using the word substitute, the steno put in the word prostitute. The boss signed the letter without reading it.

The registrar, who had scores to settle with the head of the department of physics, decided to cash in on the error. He wrote back: 'Please refer to your letter dated——The commodity asked for by you is not readily available in the store of the University. You are advised to procure the same from the market and forward the bill to the Administrative Officer.'

Another clerk applying for leave sent the following note to his boss: 'My wife is unwell. As I am the only husband in the house, kindly grant me leave for the day.'

❐

Gujaratis have a problem pronouncing the word 'wrap' and usually render it 'rape'.

Kannadigas go one better; they spell the word the way our Gujju friends pronounce it. A Hari Prakash of Bangalore writes of an accountant of a local weekly who, when the publication was delayed, had to hire casual labour to wrap magazines in brown paper for posting. In the cash payment voucher he entered the explanation, 'Paid to casual labour towards raping charges'. If the work load was heavy, the entry often read, 'Paid to casual labour towards raping throughout the night'.

❏

A professor was conducting practical tests for medical students. There were five male students before him, all of whom were duffers. The doctor kept a model of a woman's womb before them and asked them to identify the organ. He gave them a clue that it was not present in him or in either of the students. After some discussions a 'brilliant' student got up and replied, 'Sir, that organ is a brain.'

❏

An American friend resident in India vouches for the veracity of this story about the Queen of England's last visit to India. A wealthy but not too well-informed industrialist of Calcutta pestered the then British High Commission to be allowed to shake hands with the Queen. The High Commissioner gave in and arranged for the Marwari to present the Queen with a bouquet of roses on the strict understanding that he would keep his mouth shut while doing so. When the great moment came, the Marwari gentleman could not contain himself and having made his salutation and presented the roses said: 'Welcome to India, Queen Mary of England!'

The High Commissioner, red in the face, hissed: 'Shut up! Anyway Queen Mary has been dead for many years.'

Unabashed the Marwari replied, 'I am sorry, my memory failed me. I should have said Queen Victoria.'

My American friend refuses to divulge the identity of the Marwari industrialist. Any guesses?

❐

After the last summit meeting between Rajiv Gandhi and President Zia-ul-Haq, the two met privately for a friendly exchange of views. 'What is your favourite hobby?' Zia-ul-Haq asked Rajiv Gandhi.

'I collect jokes people tell about me,' replied Rajiv. 'And what is your favourite hobby, Mr President?'

'I collect people who tell jokes about me,' replied Zia-ul-Haq.

❏

A visitor to the capital approached a man at a bus stand and asked, 'Sir, will this bus go to Connaught Place?'

'Ya,' replied the man.

Not understanding what the word meant he asked another who likewise replied, 'Ya.' So did the third and the fourth man. Then he approached a Sardarji and asked the same question. He replied, 'Yes sir, it does.'

The visitor further asked, 'What does "Ya" mean? Why did you reply "yes sir"? '

'Sir ji, an educated person always says "yes sir". Only the uneducated say "ya", ' replied the Sardarji.

'Are you an educated person?'

'Ya.'

❒

Question: Why do Indian men make such lousy lovers?

Answer: They get all the love they want from their mothers and by the time they attain puberty they become emotionally impotent.

❒

Every time I go to Pakistan I pick up some jokes about its head of state, most of them about his uncanny ability to outlast political opponents and his sense of public relations. Zia is an Arain—a caste of market gardeners who grow vegetables. It is said that having retired from his onerous duties, Zia was looking for something to do which would add to his pension. An old friend who knew Zia was an Arain, suggested that since he owned a lot of land they would go into growing vegetables on a 50-50 basis. 'You do the work; what grows above the ground is yours, what grows below will be mine!'

Zia readily agreed and planted seeds of potatoes, radishes, carrots. He got the sale price of the entire crop.

His partner felt chagrined. 'Next crop, I take all that grows below the ground and you take all that grows above it.'

Zia agreed. This time he planted cauliflowers, cucumbers, peas. Once more he got all the proceeds of the sale.

The time came for the third planting. This time the landowner was determined not to lose in the bargain. 'Whatever grows below the earth and above is mine; only the middle portion will be yours,' he said.

Zia agreed. And this time he planted sugarcane. The roots below and leaves on top went to the landowner; the middle portion which has all the juice fell to Zia's share.

☐

Telegrams were sent out inviting members of the party to attend the Congress centenary celebrations in Delhi.

Some telegraph clerks not familiar with the English language changed the word centenary to 'sanitary'. Another variation of the word was used by Prakash Patil, son of Vasantdada Patil, then the chief minister of Maharashtra. When questioned whether his father had really met Prime Minister Rajiv Gandhi, he replied in the affirmative: 'Yes, at the century celebrations.'

Then there was a member of Parliament who having spoken on the budget was correcting the transcript of his speech taken down verbatim. He lost his temper and exploded: 'These fellows who prepare our Hansard get simple words wrong. I was talking on the baajet and they have taken it down as budget, not once but every time.'

A husband and wife were quarrelling. The wife got up in a temper, stuffed a few saris in her bag and was marching out of the house when the husband yelled at her, 'Where do you think you are going?'

'I am going to hell,' she hissed back.

'In that case don't forget to say my *namaskaar* to your parents and relatives.'

❐

A maternity home housed in the first floor of a multi-storeyed building had, on the ground floor, a dry-cleaner boasting of one-day service. Came a terrible dust storm which knocked down the maternity home's signboard. It fell on the dry-cleaner's, obliterating all of it except the bottom line. After the storm had blown over the two signboards read collectively as follows:

Mamta Maternity Home. Delivery within 24 hours.

❐

A devout old Christian lay on his deathbed. Instead of a priest, he summoned his lawyer and his doctor and asked them to stand on either side of his bed. 'Why do you want us beside you at this time?' they asked. Replied the dying man: 'I want to die like Jesus Christ on the cross with two thieves on either side.'

❐

An income-tax officer (in-charge of administration) in Calcutta often faced the problem of late attendance of staff. With a view to finding out the reason, he added a column in the attendance register: 'Reason for late arrival'. It did not improve matters. The staff got into the habit of inventing excuses for coming late. If the first latecomer entered against his name: 'Delayed due to late arrival of local train or traffic jam', other latecomers simply wrote 'Ditto' against their names. One day a lady stenographer arrived late by twenty minutes and wrote, 'Went to consult lady doctor for maternity problems'. Other persons who came late that day dutifully put down 'Ditto', 'Ditto' . . .

❐

A Sardarji farmer had saved up a lot of money to buy a car. But when he had the required sum, instead of buying a car he bought a buffalo. 'Sardarji, you were always saying you wanted a car to drive to the *mandi*. And now you have gone and bought another buffalo. Won't you look ridiculous riding a buffalo to the market?'

Quite unabashed, the Sardarji replied, 'Wouldn't I look more ridiculous trying to milk a Maruti?'

❏

A biology teacher was dissecting a frog. Having explained the inner features of amphibians, he asked his students, 'What would you expect to find if you dissected a human being?'

A bright lad replied, 'Sir, I would expect to find myself behind bars.'

❏

A visitor having tea at a restaurant complained about the quality of the tea.

'Sahib, we have got this tea from Darjeeling,' explained the waiter.

'Is that why it is so cold?' asked the customer.

❑

A dhobi won the first prize in a lottery and bought himself a small, electrically-run laundrette. Since he had spent his entire winnings on the machine, he retained his donkey for collecting and delivering clothes. Unfortunately, due to some fault in his meter, the dhobi's first electricity bill was so huge that he had to sell his donkey to pay it.

A short while afterwards, someone asked the donkey as to who was responsible for his master-of-many-years selling him. The donkey replied, in a loud, angry bray: 'DESU! DESU! DESU!'

❐

A   Muslim couple arrived in paradise and approached Allah for permission to have another nikaah performed. Allah asked them to wait for some time. After waiting for some years, they again approached the Almighty with their request. Allah took them to his office and showed them a pile of thousands of pending applications asking for permssion for a repeat marriage. 'You see, I can do nothing till some mullah is allowed to enter paradise; there hasn't been one for many decades.'

A delegation of Sikhs called on the former Prime Minister Rajiv Gandhi. 'The police always makes us Sikhs stand in the background at your public meetings. All other communities are given VIP treatment and allowed to stand in front,' they complained.

The former Prime Minister reassured them, 'Don't worry, as soon as we have a war on our hands, I'll see that you Sikhs are put in the front of all other communities.'

❏

Trying to show off your familiarity with foreign languages can land you in difficulties. There is the well-known case of a British minister on a visit to Moscow who, in order to please his hosts, mugged up a short speech in Russian. On his way to the banquet he realized he did not know the Russian for 'ladies and gentlemen'. He stopped his car near a public lavatory and took down the Russian equivalent. His speech did not get the kind of applause he expected. Afterwards he asked one of his colleagues what had gone wrong. The colleague replied, 'Your speech was excellent. But why did you have to start with "Male and female urinals"?'

❐

This anecdotes relates to Maulana Shaukat Ali's close association with Mahatma Gandhi during the days of the

Khilafat agitation and their subsequent parting of ways.

Gandhiji often addressed meetings from Khilafat platforms. Audiences which were largely composed of Muslims wanted to know why a Hindu bania had taken up the cause of the Caliphate which was entirely a Muslim affair. Being a tall and stout man, Maulana Shaukat Ali would have a dig at Gandhiji: 'He is a small man; I have him in my pocket.'

Later Shaukat Ali quit the Congress and joined the Muslim League. 'Where is that Mahatma Gandhi who had promised to get us Muslims our rights?' Maulana Shaukat Ali would ask at every public meeting. The Mahatma replied to the question at one of his prayer meetings: 'The Maulana wants to know where I am. He used to say he had me in his pocket. Let him look inside and he will find me.'

Agha Shahid Ali, a Delhi-born Kashmiri, is almost unknown as a poet in his homeland. He deserves to be taken seriously. I give two samples of his composition. This one is entitled, 'Today, Talk is Cheap. Call Somebody . . .'

I called Information Desk, Heaven, and
     asked, 'When is Doomsday?'
I was put on hold.
Through the hallelujahs of seraphs, I heard
     the idle gossip of angels,
Their wings beating rumours of revolts in
     Heaven.
Then I heard flames, wings burning, then
     only hallelujahs.
I prayed, Angel of love,
Please pick up the phone.
But it was the Angel of Death. I said,
     'Tell me,
Tell me, when is Doomsday?'
He answered, 'God is busy.

He never answers the living.
He has no answers for the dead.
Don't ever call again, collect.'

In another poem 'Language Games', he
has witty-macabre lines like:
You challenged me to charades.
I agreed. This would be my syllable-cure.
Tableau One: I licked a saucer of milk.
You cried: CAT!
Tableau Two: I was stubborn as a mule.
You cried: ASS.
Tableau Three: I gave you my smile, like
    a prize.
You cried: TROPHY.
You cried: CAT-ASS-TROPHY?

❒

There is an interesting episode on
Nehru's life recounted by J.K. Galbraith

who was the US ambassador in Delhi. A much-married Hollywood filmstar called on the Prime Minister.

'Well, Miss Dickinson,' Nehru said, 'when you are featured in a movie that takes two months or more to film, I suppose you become deeply involved in the role you are playing. Does that have a lasting effect on your character or personality?'

Nehru was delighted with Angie's reply: 'In my last three movies,' she said, 'I have played the part of a woman of questionable morality. I hope that has not permanently affected me.'

❐

A poor man sat outside a temple begging

for alms from worshippers: 'In the name of *Bhagwan* give this hungry man some paise to fill his belly. *Bhagwan* will bless you.' But the people went to pray in the house of God, gave the beggar so little that he never had enough to buy *daal-roti*. In sheer disgust he quit the temple and sat outside where people came for their evening shot of country liquor. 'A few paise in the name of *Bhagwan*,' he whined, as people came out in high spirits. Instead of paise many dropped rupee notes in his begging bowl. The beggar gave thanks to God in the following words: 'Hey *Bhagwan*: truly inscrutable are Thy ways! You give one address but live in another place.'

❐

Signboards on highways:

Mountains are a pleasure; only if you drive with leisure.

Drive with care, make accidents rare.

Your hurry may cause my family worry.

Always alert, accidents avert
Keep your nerves on a sharp curve.

Drive on horsepower, not on rumpower.

Darling I want you but not so fast.

❏

A Haryanvi peasant who was charged with theft went to engage a lawyer. 'How much money have you got to pay my fee?' asked the lawyer.

'*Gareeb aadmee hoon, sahib*—Sir, I am a

poor man. All I have is a tractor,' replied the peasant.

'If you have a tractor, you can't be very poor. You can raise money on it and pay me,' said the lawyer. 'What have you been accused of stealing?'

'Sir, the tractor.'

☐

There was a Punjabi couple who were connoisseurs of good food. They were invited to a dinner party by a friend. The man knew some English: his wife none at all. On their way back home after dinner the wife made disparaging remarks about the quality of the food in Punjabi: '*Palak-paneer* was *thud* (third) class. Even the *Gajar ka halva* was like *kicchad* (mud).'

Her husband agreed with her opinion. 'Nothing was good except the catering.'

'*Accha*,' replied the wife, '*Oh tay main chakkhia hee nahin*—I didn't so much as taste the catering.'

❐

A minister was the chief guest at the finals of a football tournament. After giving away the prizes, he was requested to say a few words. He said, 'It pains me to learn that this year only two teams could make it to the finals. When we have hundreds of football clubs in the country, we should endeavour to see that many more teams reach the finals next year.'

❐

Once upon a time there was a preacher who wanted to collect money for the church. He was told that horse-racing was the quickest way of getting it. So he went to a horse auction but finding the bids too high, bought himself an ass. He entered it in the local races. To everyone's surprise the donkey came in third. The next morning, the papers had headlines on their sports pages reading: 'Preacher's ass steals show.'

Encouraged by the donkey's performance, the preacher entered it for the next race. It romped in first. The next morning's papers carried the headlines: 'Preacher's ass in front.'

The bishop was outraged and ordered the preacher to get rid of the animal. The preacher dutifully gave it to a nun. The papers heard of it and reported the event in the headlines: 'Nun has the best ass in town.'

This time the bishop was furious and ordered the nun to dispose of the animal. She sold it to a farmer for ten dollars. The next day, the papers reported: 'Nun peddles ass for ten bucks.'

❏

The signboard on the door of a lawyer's chamber reads: 'Where there is a will there is a way; where there is a way there is law; where there is law there is a rule; where there is a rule there is a loophole; where there is a loophole there is a lawyer; and here I am Mr . . ., advocate.'

❏

R.E. Canteenwala gets malicious pleasure in translating foreign names to get a laugh. A Chinese friend named Who Flung Dung was addressed as 'Flying lump of shit'. Most unkind!

Names in one language can often be uncomplimentary in another. Canteenwala should know that the common Indian surname, Das, means turd in Swedish. The commonest Scandinavian surname, Lund, and the name of the German Parliament, Bund, refer to the fore and aft of the human anatomy in Hindustani. Then there was the South Korean ambassador, who later became foreign minister, whose name was Bum Suk Lee. What about Canteenwala? How would it sound as *bawarchikhaneyka*? His own community, the Bawajis, provide the funniest sounding names in India.

A person, looking for a house, contacted a property dealer. The only house available at a reasonable rent was known as '*Bhoot Bangla*'. The man got the address, proceeded to the house and rang the bell. Two men came out. The househunter asked, 'Sir, is it true that this house is haunted?' The two persons looked at each other and replied: 'You better ask someone living nearby; we died more than fifty years ago.'

❐

Banta Singh was living in a DDA ground floor flat with his 12 children. A family planning motivator called on him and asked him somewhat acidly, 'Banta Singhji, how is it that you have so many children?'

'*Sab ooper vaaley dee mayta hai*—it's all the gift of the One above—' he replied, pointing to the roof.

The family planning man promptly went to the first floor, got hold of Santa Singh who occupied the premises and had his *nasbandi* done.

❐

A couple of weeks ago I received an anonymous letter from Islamabad containing an unsigned poem entitled, 'A User's Guide to Indian Causology'. I found it extremely witty and biting in its satire. I reproduce it in full for Indian readers.

When the monsoon fails and the sun
  drums down
On the parched Gangetic plain

And the tanks dry up and dust storms
  blow
Where once were fields of grain
When hunger stalks each village hut
And famine grips the land,
It isn't Mother Nature's fault—
It is the Foreign Hand!
For this is India, you see,
Not Germany or France,
And nothing here is blamed on God
Much less on quirky chance.
Here evil has a fingered form
Both alien and planned
It is that darkly subtle limb—
It is the Foreign Hand!
When Hindu lads hack Sikhs to death
In peaceful Delhi town
When Rajiv's corns are acting up
Or the Bombay bourse goes down,
When the pesky little Nepalese
Insist on things like borders

When once-tame Tamil Tigers balk
At taking South Block orders
The reasons for this mischief
I think you'll understand
It's those meddling foreign digits—
It is the Foreign Hand!
So when you're in a Delhi lift
Beside a buxom dame
And you give in to the natural urge
To pinch her husky frame,
Confront her adamantine glare
With a visage mildly bland,
And say: 'It wasn't me, my dear—
It was the Foreign Hand!'

❏

When Kamraj Nadar was Congress
President, he used to come to Delhi to

attend meetings, conferences etc. When in Delhi, he used to stay with Pandit Nehru. During the course of breakfast, lunch, dinner etc. Kamraj Nadar used to impress upon Pandit Nehru the comfort of wearing *lungis*. 'It is very convenient for going to the bathroom and walking in the garden, lying down in bed etc.' He promised to send a dozen *lungis* to Pandit Nehru from Madras.

Pandit Nehru got angry and replied: 'Mr Nadar, *lungis* are for you South Indians. If I wore a *lungi*, how will I do *shirshasana*?'

❏

A gentleman, very proud of his wit, while leaving for office used to say to his wife: 'Good-bye, oh Mother of four!'

One morning, his wife, who had had enough, retorted: 'Ta ta! Father of two!'

That ended the husband's witticisms.

❏

Here are examples of some charming misprints. In Pune, a devout truck driver has printed behind his vehicle: 'God is grate'. And a butcher advertises his wares as 'Farash meet of Pork sold here'.

The best is the signboard on a bakery:

'Bakery Number One
Dilruba & Sons
The biggest loafers in town.'

❏

On a rain-soaked night, an infant

tumbled over the railings of the Howrah bridge and fell into the Hooghly river below. The weather did not prevent hundreds of Calcuttans from flocking to the spot and watching the proceedings, but no one attempted to save the drowning child. At last an old American tourist jumped into the water and did the saving. Later, when he was being interviewed by the radio and TV, complimented on his bravery and asked to say something, he roared at them saying, 'Bring forward the rascal who pushed me from behind.'

❒

Once a couple had one of their usual quarrels; as a consequence of which, they stopped talking to each other.

Unfortunately the husband was to attend his office very early the next morning. So he wrote on a piece of paper, 'Please wake me up at 6 a.m. tomorrow morning,' and kept it beside his wife's pillow.

His wife read it and went to sleep.

He woke up very late the next morning and got very angry. He looked ferociously at his wife, but she calmly pointed towards his pillow. Under his pillow he found a piece of paper. On it was written, 'Please wake up, it is 6 o'clock now.'

❐

A Sardar walked into a household appliances store. The owner was busy tallying his accounts and his eyes were glued to his ledgers. The Sardar told the owner, 'I want that VCR.' Without taking his eyes off the ledgers, the owner replied, 'No, Sardar, that is not for you.'

Our Sardar felt insulted. He thought that the shopkeeper was biased against Sardars. Next day, he arrived at the shop clean-shaven and without his headgear. He asked for the same VCR. The owner, who was again busy tallying his accounts replied without raising his head, 'No, Sardar, that is not for you.'

The Sardar was perplexed. How could the shopkeeper guess correctly that he was a Sardar? So, the next day, he went to the same shop disguised as a woman, in *churidar* and *pyjama*, head covered with *dupatta*, and asked for the same VCR. The shopkeeper again replied without raising his head—'No, Sardar, that is not for you!'

Puzzled, the Sardar asked the shopkeeper how he guessed that he was a

Sardar without raising his head. 'Very simple,' said the shopkeeper. 'That is not a VCR. That is a washing machine!'

□

A mother and her convent-raised young daughter were riding in a taxi one evening through a midtown block notorious for street solicitation. 'What are all these women waiting for, mother?' the girl asked.

'They're probably meeting their husbands after work,' replied the woman hastily.

'Aw, c'mon lady,' grumbled the taxi-driver, 'why don'tcha tell her the truth? She's old enough.'

'Please mom,' said the girl, 'I want to know.'

Looking daggers at the back of the driver's head, the woman carefully explained the situation. When she had finished, the daughter asked, 'But, what happens to the babies those women have?'

'They grow up,' the woman replied, 'and become taxi-drivers.'

❏

Emperor Akbar was bending down to pick up a couple of coins that had dropped from his pockets when Birbal tiptoed behind him and administered a harmless tap on the royal behind. The king leaped up, and flew into such a rage that he ordered Birbal's execution. When he calmed down slightly, however, he announced that Birbal would be given his freedom if he could come up with an excuse more outrageous than the original act.

Birbal promptly said, 'As a matter of fact, I didn't know it was you—I thought it was the Queen.'

❐

This refers to an IAS officer who could read, write and even speak English. He once gave a 'very good' report of his subordinate officer, writing in his confidential report that the officer 'hardly works'. It was only after the officers' representation that the reporting officer clarified that he meant the officer was hardworking. When the same officer once went to inspect a BSF picket on Gurdaspur border, he made these brief remarks on the Visitors' Book: 'Jawans are healthy, horses are happy, I am glad.'

❐

Once a Jat went to Bombay. Going down a road he saw a very high building. He was amazed by it, and decided to count its storeys. As he was doing so a townsman saw him and decided to fool him. So he approached the Jat and asked, 'What are you doing?' When he was told the answer the townsman said that one had to pay two rupees for every storey counted. 'How many have you counted?' The Jat said ten and gave the man twenty rupees. As he walked away, the Jat smiled to himself, happy at the thought that he had fooled the other man, for he had actually counted twenty.

□

A notorious tiger was on the prowl, terrorizing a village. So the villagers held a high level meeting to put down this menace. A brave Sardarji stood up twisting his moustache and flexing his muscles. 'I can tackle this maneater single-handed,' he boasted. 'Give me a cowhide,' he roared, 'and remember, not a single soul should venture out tonight. Leave the rest to me.' That night, disguised as a cow he stood as a bait waiting to ambush the tiger. Hours passed; suddenly the villagers heard someone screaming in great agony. They all dashed to the spot, only to find the Sardarji lying on the ground groaning and bleeding profusely. One of them asked the Sardarji, 'What's the matter? Did you manage to kill the tiger?' Already some of the villagers had begun shouting, 'Sardarji *zindabad*, Sardarji *zindabad*.'

'Stop it you idiots! Traitors!' he screamed. 'Tell me first whose bull was it, whose bull was loose tonight!'

❑

An American and a Russian were arguing about the virtues of communism and democracy.

'C'mon man!' said the American, 'in a democracy you get to express your views. You have freedom. You know, I can anyday call President Bush an idiot!'

'What's so great about that,' said the Russian, unimpressed, 'so can I!'

❏

A Sardarji went to the doctor to get some medicine as he was not feeling well. 'This is pretty strong stuff,' said the doctor, 'so take some the first day, then skip a day, take some again on the third day and then skip another day and so on.'

A few months later the doctor met the Sardarji's wife and asked how he was.

'Oh, he is dead,' she told him.

'Did not the medicine I prescribed do him any good?' asked the doctor.

'Oh, the medicine was all right,' she replied. 'It was all that skipping that killed him.'

One night, Banta was walking homewards when a thief sprang at him all of a sudden. Banta and the thief had a terrific tussle. They rolled about on the ground, and Banta put up a tremendous fight until, at last, the thief managed to get the better of him and pinned him to the ground.

The thief then went through Banta's pockets and searched him all over. There was only 25 paise coin he could lay his hands on. The thief was so surprised at this that he asked Banta why he had bothered to fight so hard just for 25 paise.

'Was that all you wanted?' said Banta Singh. 'I thought you were after the five hundred rupees I've got in my shoe!'

After a number of years in England Natha Singh returned to visit his native village in Punjab. But he decided first to spend a few days in Bombay, and then a day in Delhi to pay homage at the Bangla Saheb Gurdwara near Connaught Place.

He landed in Bombay and a friend received him. He enjoyed his sightseeing in Bombay and after a couple of days boarded a train for Delhi. He went into deep sleep in the train. The train reached Bhopal at about 8 a.m. Someone in the compartment switched on radio. And the Hindi newsreader's voice said, *'Yeh Dilli hai'*. This woke Natha Singh up. He got up hurriedly, collected his bags, got down and went out of the railway station. He got into a cycle rickshaw and told the man to go take him to Bangla Saheb Gurdwara near Connaught Place. Now this clever Muslim rickshaw-puller of Bhopal smiled to himself, and was on his way.

After two hours the rickshaw-puller, with a worried look, told Natha Singh that he had lost his way and would need to ask someone for directions. Then he got off and went to a nearby teastall, where he took his time over a glass of tea, joking with another rickshaw-puller about his stupid passenger.

In the meanwhile Natha Singh was getting nervous and impatient. Luckily, he saw another Sardarji coming his way in a rickshaw. Natha Singh ran towards him and requested him to alight and listen to him in private.

This Sardarji nodded wisely and got down and listened to Natha Singh's woes.

Natha Singh explained in a whisper: 'You know, my rickshaw-puller seems to be a rogue. He has been taking me for a ride. Two hours ago I started in his rickshaw from the railway station for Connaught Place to go to Bangla Saheb Gurdwara and now he says he has lost his way.'

'You have become impatient in two hours?' said the other Sardarji. 'I have been in my rickshaw for the last ten hours and my rickshaw-puller has still not reached Karol Bagh.'

❐

A general, a colonel and a major were having a heated argument on the subject of sex. The general maintained that sex was 60 per cent work and 40 per cent fun. The colonel said it was 75 per cent work and 25 per cent fun. The major thought it was 90 per cent work and 10 per cent fun.

At the height of the argument, a private appeared at the door.

'Let's leave it to him,' said the major.

The private listened carefully and said with an air of absolute finality, 'If you will pardon me, sirs, sex is 100 per cent fun and no work at all.'

'How do you figure that?' cried the astonished officers.

'It is very simple,' said the private. 'If there was any work in it at all, you guys would have me doing it for you.'

❑

Sign outside a tutorial school in Meerut Cantonment: 'Expert Kotching in English given here.'

Notice in a DTC bus: 'Eve-teasing is an offence. Passengers are requested to cooperate.'

Outside a department store in Connaught Place: 'Please note that we shall not be responsible for any rotten stuff unless it bears our label.'

A store advertising a new brand of cough syrup: 'Got a cold? Try our cough drops. We guarantee you'll never get better.'

Sign in Hindi outside a theka *(liquor vend) in Meerut:* 'If you drink to forget everything, kindly pay us in advance.'

On the rear window of a car (en route to Dehradun from Meerut): Always drive in such a way that your licence expires before you do.'

❑

When dying, Mr Smith told his wife, 'Be faithful to my memory or I shall turn in my grave.' A year later Mrs Smith reached her heavenly abode and enquired about her husband. 'Mr Smith?' Gabriel told her, 'Madam, there are a million Smiths here. Is there anything more you can relate to help identify him?' 'Oh, yes, my husband said he would turn in his grave if I was not faithful to his memory,' Mrs Smith replied. 'Oh! you mean spinning-wheel Smith.'

❐

A young lady went to a hospital and told the receptionist that she wished to see an upturn. 'You mean an intern, don't you dear?' asked the kindly nurse. 'Well, whatever you call it . . . I want a contamination,' replied the girl. 'You mean examination,' corrected the nurse. 'Maybe so,' allowed the girl. 'I want to go to the fraternity ward.' 'Maternity ward,' said the nurse with a slight smile. 'Look,' insisted the girl, 'I don't know much about big words, but I do know that I haven't demonstrated for two months, and I think I'm stagnant.'

❑

A news item in an American newspaper: 'Thieves escaped with over half a million dollars from a bank last night. Police are baffled trying to figure out the motive for the crime.'

❑

A photographer was called to take a picture of a deceased person. After focussing he asked the son of the deceased person to remove the cloth from the face and said, 'Smile please!'

❐

A rich man on his deathbed asked his wife to bury him without any clothes on. 'I know which way I'm going,' he explained. 'I won't need clothes up there!'

When he passed away, his wife kept her promise. A few days later, just as the widow was preparing to go to bed one evening, the man's ghost appeared through the window and said, 'Get out my winter underwear and my tweed overcoat, darling. There are so many rich people in Hell now, they've installed air-conditioning.'

After Rekha married Mukesh Agarwal, her chief rival in the film world, Sridevi, was eager to outdo her. She received a proposal from a handsome business magnate of the name of Mr Lal. Sridevi turned down the proposal without bothering to even look at the man. When asked the reason why she had done so, she replied, 'I don't wish to be known as Sri Devi Lal.'

❏

Two rival authors met. One had just published a book. Said the other, 'I read your book and thought it was great. Tell me, who wrote it for you?'

The author replied, 'I'm so glad you enjoyed it. Tell me, who read it for you?'

A father was worried about his son's ability to pass his English essay test. So he made him cram one on 'My Best Friend' which he was sure would be one of the choices. Instead of that the subject on the examination paper was 'My Father'. Undaunted, the boy utilized his memorized text to his best advantage. His essay read: 'I have many fathers. Ravi Prasad is my best father. He lives next door to us. He comes to visit us every day. My mother loves him very much. A father in need is a father indeed.'

❏

Two men who had recently emigrated to a foreign country were boasting about their skill in fooling others. 'None can surpass me in this art,' said Lehna Singh.

'How is that?' asked Banta Singh.

'I have fooled the government,' replied Lehna Singh. 'I've come to this country on a return ticket and I am not going back,' he added, with a twinkle in his eye.

A gambler's three-year-old son learnt to count upto thirteen. It went as follows: *Ek, do, teen, chaar, paanch, chhey, saat, aath, nau, das, ghulam, begam, badshah.*

❏

Diplomat: A person who thinks twice before saying nothing.

Politician: Someone who shakes your hand before the elections—and your confidence afterwards.

Husband: A person who is under the impression that he bosses the house when in reality he only houses the boss.

Television: A chatter-box that presents programmes that give you a headache and then advertises a cure for it.

Chaperon: An elderly woman who accompanies young women to ensure that they don't commit any such mistake as she committed when she herself was young.

An economist: Someone who thinks more about money than the people who have it.

Childhood: When you make funny faces in the mirror.

Middle age: When the mirror gets even.

❏

Epitaph on a rich man's tomb: 'I struggled with arithmetic all my life. As a child, I learned to add. As a young man, I was a master at multiplying. As an adult I never learned to subtract. And now my relatives will divide.'

□

At a Christmas Carol Service number of officials were invited to read selected portions from the Scriptures. One portion— 'The treasures will be opened and the glories of God will be revealed'—was read as: 'The trousers will be opened and the glories of God will be revealed'.

□

A middle-aged woman went to see her doctor. 'Well, what's the trouble?' he asked.

'Doctor, it's this terrible headache; shooting pains in my legs and high blood pressure.'

'How old are you?' asked the doctor.

'I'll be twenty-six on my next birthday.'

'H'mm,' said the doctor, busy writing, 'loss of memory too.'

❐

Mr and Mrs Banta Singh's two-year-old boy was bawling away loudly. Mrs Singh asked her husband why their son was being so difficult. 'He wants to take a ride on a donkey,' replied Banta.

'Then why don't you put him on your shoulders and go for a run?'

❐

A shopkeeper's son had trouble with his eyes. He took the boy to an eye-specialist who operated on the boy and replaced his eyes with those donated by a minister.

A few days after the operation, the doctor asked the father, 'How's your son doing?'

'He is fine,' replied the father, 'but he keeps on gazing at a chair whenever he finds one.'

❑

Santa Singh and Banta Singh were always boasting of their parents' achievements to each other.

Santa Singh: 'Have you heard of the Suez Canal?'

Banta Singh: 'Yes, I have.'

Santa Singh: 'Well, my father dug it.'

Banta Singh: 'That's nothing. Have you heard of the Dead Sea?'

Santa Singh: 'Yes, I have.'

Banta Singh: 'Well, my father killed it.'

❑

A Sardarji went to a logic school to learn logic. 'To begin with, I'll explain logic to you with the help of an example,' the Professor said.

'Do you have a fish pond?' asked the Professor.

'Yes,' said Sardarji.

'This means you love fish,' the Professor continued.

'Yes.'

'That is you love water.'

'Yes.'

'Everybody drinks water, so you love everybody.'

'Yes.'

'And if you love everybody, you love girls.'

'Yes.'

'If you love girls, then you are a boy.'

'Yes, I am a boy.'

'And if you are a boy and you love girls, you are not homosexual.'

'Yes, true, I am not a homosexual,' said Sardarji.

'So this is the logical relationship between a fish pond and a homosexual,' the Professor ended.

That night Sardarji could not sleep well and wondered about the logical relationship between a fish pond and a homosexual. Next day, on his way to the logic school, he met a friend who enquired about his first day at logic school. Sardarji said proudly, 'I'll explain logic to you with the help of an example.'

'Do you have a fish pond?' asked Sardarji.

'No,' his friend replied.

'Then you are a homosexual,' Sardarji concluded.

❏

A man set down three pieces of luggage before the Indian Airlines check-in counter at the Santa Cruz Airport, Bombay. 'I want the brown bag to go to Delhi, the black one to Calcutta,' he said. 'And keep the third bag here till I come back next week and pick it up.'

The airline official blinked. A supervisor standing behind the check-in clerk overheard the passenger's request and came up. 'I am sorry, but we are not the post office,' the supervisor said, 'we can't do that.'

'Why not?' the irate passenger said, raising his voice: 'That's what you did the last time!'

❐

In the Garden of Eden, Adam asked God, 'Why did you make Eve so beautiful?'

'To attract your attention.'

'Why did you give her such a winsome personality?'

'So that you would love her.'

Adam thought about this for a while.

'Why, then did you make her so
dumb?'

'So that she would love you!'

❏

A policeman bitten by a dog came for
treatment to the Safdarjang Hospital. He
asked the pharmacist, '*Arey bhai! Kuttey
katne kee davaa dena*—brother, give me
medicine for dog bite.'

The pharmacist asked him, '*Santree
jee! Aap ko bhee kuttey nay kaat liya*—how
did a dog bite a policeman?'

The constable replied, 'To tell you
the truth, I was not wearing my uniform at
the time.'

❏

Mrs Banta knitted a sweater and sent it to her husband by parcel post. With it she sent the following note: 'I have removed the buttons as they are too heavy and would add to the price of postage. You will find them in the right hand pocket of the sweater.'

❐

Santa and Banta got jobs in Dubai. They also found accommodation in a high-rise building: Santa on the ground floor, Banta on the twenty-fifth. One day when the lift was not working, Banta invited Santa for dinner in his twenty-fifth floor flat. Poor Santa trudged up the twenty-five floors only to find Banta's flat locked and a big board on the door which read: 'How did you enjoy your dinner?'

Not to be outdone, Santa wrote under the board, 'Sorry, I could not make it.'

❏

Mrs Banta shouted at her servant: '*Oi bewakoof*, this egg is ice cold. Did you boil it in iced water?'

❏

A young man was ogling at a middle-aged lady. She got angry and ticked him off. The young man pleaded, 'Madam, you are exactly like my mother.'

'That is not possible,' retorted the lady angrily. 'I happen to be a married woman.'

❏

Banta complained to a friend, 'My wife never agrees with anything: I say, and we have been married six years.'

Mrs Banta intervened, 'Not six; we have been married for seven years!'

❐

Teacher: 'What is the scientific formula for water?'

Bright pupil: 'H.I.J.K.L.M.N.O.'

Teacher: 'Nonsense! How did you arrive at that?'

Bright pupil: 'Auntie, it is H to O (H_2O)!'

❐

An unmarried girl prayed, '*Hey Bhagwan*, I never asked you for anything. But please grant my mother a son-in-law.'

Bhagwan heard the girl's prayer. Her sister found a husband!

❑

A man rang up a bookstore and said, 'Please send me all the books you have by Khushwant Singh. Also send me something to read.'

❑

The traditional blessing *Satputri hoven* (may you be the mother of seven) had a bizarre denouement: a young lady with her face hidden behind her veil touched the feet of an older woman to seek her blessing. '*Satputri hoven*,' said the old woman.

The blessing-seeker uncovered her face and retorted, 'And what do you expect me to do to my eighth? Poison him?'

❐

An old bishop in the nation's capital was sick of the social and embassy parties he was expected to attend every other afternoon. At one of them he entered wearily, glanced sourly at the over-familiar cast of characters and sank into the nearest chair. The hostess coyly said, 'A spot of tea, Bishop?'

'No tea,' growled the bishop.

'Coffee, Bishop?'

'No coffee.'

An understanding woman, she whispered in his ear, 'Scotch and water, Bishop?'

Said the bishop, brightening, 'No water!'

❏

A young couple moved recently into the neighbourhood. Every morning, the Mukherjees watched the young woman kiss her husband goodbye as he left for the day.

One day, looking enviously across the fence, Mrs Mukherjee asked her husband: 'Don't you ever feel like doing that?' Her husband replied hesitatingly: 'Uh! I sure do, but I don't know how the young man will react.'

❏

Doctor: 'Considering the weak state of your eyes, I would suggest it would be good for you to gaze into empty space.'

Patient: 'Thank you, Doc. I'll keep looking into my wallet.'

❐

Bal Thackeray, while visiting the largest government hospital in Bombay, asked a houseman what he was doing.

'Administering local anaesthetic,' said the surgeon.

'*Shabash*,' exclaimed the Shiv Sena supremo, 'you see, we certainly don't need those non-local anaesthetics in Maharashtra any more!'

❐

Sardar Banta Singh arrived at the Indira
Gandhi International Airport with his wife
and four children, and checked in to catch
their flight to Abu Dhabi where he had
been promised a good job. While waiting
for the flight to be called, Banta Singh
looked round the departure lounge and
saw a machine full of coloured bulbs. On
it flashed a panel stating: *Insert 10-paise
coin and learn the truth.*

Banta inserted a 10-paise coin. The
machine made a whirring sound and out
came a ticket. It read: *Your name is Sardar
Banta Singh. You are waiting to catch a flight
to Abu Dhabi.*

Banta Singh was very excited and
beckoned to his family. Mrs Banta inserted
a 10-paise coin. The machine again made
a whirring noise and out came another
ticket reading: *Your name is Sardarni Banta
Singh and you are waiting to catch your flight
to Abu Dhabi.*

In turn the children put in 10-paise coins and got the same answer. After they had finished, Banta Singh thought he would try the machine one last time. He inserted a coin. The machine whirred and out came another ticket reading: *Your name is Sardar Banta Singh and you have just missed your flight to Abu Dhabi!*

❐

Sir Arthur Conan Doyle, author of the Sherlock Holmes stories, was convinced that the dead could communicate with the living. Once, shortly after the death of a fellow writer, he was asked if he had heard from the deceased. He admitted that he had not.

'Are you convinced now,' continued

his questioner, 'that spiritualism is a fake?'

'Not at all,' replied Doyle, 'I hadn't expected him to contact me. We weren't on speaking terms when he died.'

❏

It was the Irish chess championship and the two Irish grandmasters were sitting with their heads bent over the board, contemplating their strategies. Radio, television and the newspapers waited with bated breath for the next move. Hours went by and there was no sign of anything happening. Then one of the grandmasters looked up and said, 'Oh, is it my move?'

❏

Passengers were scrambling out of a crowded train when a female voice suddenly brought everything to a halt. 'Just a minute,' she called out, 'let me take off my clothes.' Everyone turned around expectantly, only to see an elderly washerwoman drag out a bundle of clothes from under her seat.

❏

The three stages of sickness:

Ill

Pill

Bill

Sometimes there is a fourth:

Will

❏

First man: 'Call me a doctor—call me a doctor!'

Second man: 'What's the matter? Are you sick?'

First man: 'No, I've just graduated from medical school!'

❐

Three persons—an American, an Englishman and a Sardarji were convicted of murder; but they were given a choice—to die by hanging, electric chair or an AIDS injection.

The Englishman opted for the first, and died. The American said he did not want to die like the Englishman with his tongue sticking out. He opted for the electric chair, and died. The Sardarji opted for the AIDS injection, so his trousers were pulled down, and he was given a big dose of the AIDS virus in his bottom.

Soon after, the Sardarji was found jumping about, singing and laughing. On being asked what he was so happy about, the Sardarji replied, 'You people thought you were very clever giving me that injection but you did not realize that I was wearing a condom at the time!'

❏

An Englishman, a Frenchman and a Russian were arguing about the nationality of Adam and Eve.

'They must have been English,' declared the Englishman. 'Only a gentleman would share his last apple with a woman.'

'They were undoubtedly French,' said the Frenchman. 'Who else could seduce a woman so easily?'

'I think they were Russians,' said the Russian. 'After all, who else could walk stark naked, feed on one apple between the two of them and think they were in Paradise?'

❐

The following is a true story: Mr S.N. Talukdar, the Director of the R&D Institute of the ONGC, and Dr V.V. Sastri, the Additional Director, were often at loggerheads as is normally the case with geologists. Mr Talukdar, son of a former ICS official in the Raj, had a fetish about neatness and enforced it in the Institute with a strong hand. One morning during his rounds through the Institute, Mr Talukdar peeped into Dr Sastri's office. Dr Sastri was not in his office at that time and Mr Talukdar observed that the room was extremely messy. He left a note saying: 'A cluttered table represents a cluttered mind,' and walked out.

Sometime later, Dr Sastri came back to his office and hit the roof on reading Mr Talukdar's note. He stormed into his superior's office to settle scores. Fortunately for him, Mr Talukdar was not in his office. That helped him to cool off.

Later in the day, when Mr Talukdar entered his office, he found the following note waiting for him on his neat table: 'If a cluttered table represents a cluttered mind, what does an empty table represent?'

❑

Democracy: Where it's your vote that counts.

Feudalism: Where it's your count that votes.

❒

A pastor phoned the municipal office to ask that a dead mule be removed from the front of the church. Said the young clerk who took the call, 'I thought you clergymen took care of the dead.'

'We do,' answered the pastor, 'but first we get in touch with their relatives!'

❒

A bus traveller in Bombay noted lady passengers buying tickets and saying, 'Kalbadevi,' 'Prabahadevi,' and the like. When the conductor approached him for a ticket, he said, 'Amirchand.'

Before his death, Stalin had given two envelopes to Khrushchev, which he was asked to open in times of emergency. For the first six years, everything went smoothly. But when Khrushchev faced problems he opened the first envelope. It read, 'Now begin to criticize me for every wrong in the state.' The trick proved successful.

Then for the next five years Khrushchev had no problems. But when he began to face problems again, he opened the second envelope. It read, 'Now it is time for you to prepare two similar envelopes and retire.'

❐

During the selections for the school football team, the coach gave the players the option of selecting their own playing positions. The players made up their minds and the coach began to ask them about their playing positions. The conversation went as follows:

Coach: 'Banerjee?'

Banerjee: 'Centre Forward, sir.'

Coach: 'Kumar?'

Kumar: 'Right Back, sir.'

Coach: 'What about you, Singh?'

Singh: 'There is a slight problem.'

Coach: 'What?'

Singh: 'My friends are wicked, they want me to play Left Out, sir.'

Coach: 'So, what's the problem?'

Singh: 'How can I play leftout? Won't I have to play outside the field, sir?'

❏

At a Miss India contest, a gentleman congratulated Sunil Gavaskar, saying, 'Indian cricket really owes a debt of gratitude to you for producing two such fine cricketers—Tendulkar and Kambli.' Hearing this, the Little Master shot back, 'You must be mistaken; I played no part in producing them. I have never been near either of their mothers.'

❒

Why did the little pony lose his voice?

Because he was a litle hoarse.

What kind of profits do fishermen make?

Net profits.

What is the language of chickens called?

Fowl language.

What happened to the cow that could

not give milk?

It was an udder failure.

What did the clumsy optician do at a party?

He made a spectacle of himself.

Why is a cross-eyed teacher not successful in class?

Because she can't control her pupils.

❐

Ajanta was a fine Botany student and good at practicals. One day in the lab, her teacher inspected her work. Very pleased at her dissection of a flower, the teacher called out to the other students, 'Come here and see Ajanta's ovary; it is so beautiful.'

❐

Son: 'Dad, who is more intelligent—a father or a son?'

Father: 'Father, of course.'

Son: 'No, it's the son who is more intelligent.'

Father: 'And how is that?'

Son: 'Okay, who discovered the steam engine?'

Father: 'James Watt.'

Son: 'Why not his dad?'

❑

Alexander The Great, Julius Caesar and Napoleon were watching a military parade in Moscow. Alexander could not take his eyes off the tanks. 'If I had chariots like these,' he said, 'I could have conquered the whole of Asia.'

Caesar eyed the missiles and said, 'With such arrows, I could have ruled the world.'

Napoleon glanced up from a copy of *Pravda* and said, 'With a newspaper like this, no one would even have heard of Waterloo!'

❏

The bald-headed barber was trying to sell a bottle of hair tonic to his customer.

'But how can you sell it, when you yourself have no hair?' he was challenged.

'Nothing wrong with that,' came the reply, 'I know a guy who sells brassiers.'

❏

A wife to her husband: 'Can you tell me the difference between Truth and Belief?'

Husband, replying thoughtfully after a short pause: 'Look, dear, "Raju is your son" is a truth; "Raju is my son" is a belief.'

❐

In most jokes about drowning, when people call on their respective gods for help, Hindu deities come off poorly. Sita Ram Goel, editor of *Voice of India* and an important mouthpiece of Hindu opinion, rectifies the balance:

Three men—a Sikh, a Musilm and a Hindu—jumped into the sea from a boat which was sinking. None of them knew how to swim. So all of them invoked their deities for help. The Sikh cried for Satguru. But the name applied to ten gurus, and they got into an argument as to which particular one was being invoked. Meanwhile, the poor Sikh sank to the bottom of the sea. The Muslim cried out to Allah. But Allah was bound by his own undertaking that He would save Momins only on the Day of Judgement which was still far off. So the hapless Muslim went down as well. The Hindu had only to utter one of the several divine names he knew and as every divine name in Hindu theology is shared in common by thirty-three crore gods, all of them rushed to his rescue. He alone survived to tell the story!

❐

Overheard: 'Just when I learnt to take the sweet things of life, the doctor stopped me from eating sugar.'

'Oh! my case is more tragic! When I learnt to take things with a grain of salt, the doctor put me on a salt-free diet.'

❏

A man having dined in a restaurant was washing his hands in the wash basin. Having done so he noticed the towel on the rack was very dirty. He went to the manager to complain.

'Sir, you have no reason to complain,' replied the manager. 'The towel has been there since the morning. Dozens of people have wiped their hands and faces with it. No one said anything about it. You are the first one to complain.'

❏

Bhalla Singh Bhatindawala went for an interview with a firm. The boss judged him on all subjects and the last subject was English. Bhalla was asked to give out the word opposite in meaning to that spoken by his boss. The test began and the boss said the first word: 'Day.' Brilliant Bhalla replied, 'Night.' 'Ugly,' said the boss. 'Pichchly,' said Bhalla, instead of saying 'pretty'.

This made the boss furious and he shouted: 'Wrong.'

'Right,' said Bhalla.

'Shut up.'

'I'll speak.'

'Get out.'

'Come in.'

'You are rejected.'

'I am selected.'

Finally, the boss gave in and appointed him.

A village tailor decamped leaving his clients in a quandary. 'He took my pant piece with him,' complained Ram Pal.

'He took my suit length with him,' complained Ilahi Baksh.

Banta Singh had a more serious complaint: '*Mera to naap lay kar bhaag gayaa*—he decamped with my measurements!'

❏

Many people are not sure how long they should wait after the birth of a child before resuming sexual intercourse. This should give them some assurance.

A man whose wife was having her first child asked the gynaecologist, 'How long after she has had the baby can we resume love-making?'

Replied the medico, 'It really depends on whether she is in a general ward or has a private room.'

❒

A man goes to the doctor complaining of hearing loss. The doctor examines him and says he wants to fix the fellow with a new hearing aid.

'This is the finest hearing aid now being manufactured. I wear one myself,' says the doctor.

'What kind is it?' asks the man.

'About half-past four!'

❒

Abuse can be an art if it is spontaneous, cool and hits the mark fairly and squarely.

A lot of abuse has been traded between leaders of political parties and their traducers. Some of it is spontaneous but typically angry and way off the mark.

Among some juicy insults is an exchange between the notorious John Wilkes and the Earl of Sandwich. Once Wilkes taunted the Earl, 'I predict, sir, that you will die by hanging or from some loathsome disease.'

Replied the Earl of Sandwich, 'That depends, my dear sir, on whether I embrace your principles or your mistress.'

Now, that is foul-mouthing with panache!

❐

A young man approached Banta for the hand of his daughter. Banta knew that the fellow earned nothing and was a loafer. 'I don't want my daughter to spend all her life with a *gadha* (donkey),' he told the suitor.

'I know,' replied the young man, 'that is why I want to marry her.'

❐

A man in Delhi made a trunk call to his old friend in Amritsar. '*Banta yarr*,' he said, 'I am in great difficulty. Can you send me Rs 500? I will return it within a month.'

'Hello! Hello!' replied Banta, 'I can't hear you. The line is very faint.'

The friend repeated more loudly, 'Send me Rs 500. I'll return it soon.'

'I can't hear a word,' replied Banta, 'you ring me another time.'

The operator who was listening, interrupted, 'The line is absolutely clear.

Your friend in Delhi wants you to send him Rs 500.'

Banta snapped back at the operator, 'If you can hear him so clearly, why don't *you* lend him Rs 500?'

❐

'What did you learn in school today?' The mother asked her young son.

'I learned how to add,' replied the child. 'Two plus two the son of a bitch is four. Three plus three the son of a bitch is six . . .'

The shocked mother went to the school the next day and confronted the teacher who, on hearing her complaint, was equally shocked. So the child was called in to repeat what he had learnt. Hearing him, the teacher burst out laughing and said, 'What I actually taught the children was two plus two, the sum of which is four; three plus three, the sum of which is six!'

❏

A young man cycling along a crowded road ran into an elderly lady accompanied by her attractive daughter. The young lady shouted at him, '*Andha hai?*' (Are you blind?)

'*Jee haan, miss sahab,*' replied the cheeky cyclist. 'I must be blind to run into the wrong lady.'

❏

Banta's wife served her husband roasted chicken for dinner. She said, 'Sardarji, I cooked this chicken in an electric stove.'

'I guessed that,' replied Banta, 'every time I take a bite I get a *jhatka*—an electric shock.'

❒

Santa and Banta met on a village road. Santa was carrying a large gunny bag over his shoulder.

'*Oye*, Santa,' hailed Banta, 'what is in the bag?'

'*Murgiyan*—chickens,' came the reply.

'If I guess how many, can I have one?' asked Banta.

'You can have both of them.'

'OK,' said Banta, 'five.'

❒

Cheer up my son, buck up my boy,
   You are living in 'The Land of Joy'.

You go to school where they do not
teach,

In the House of God, they hatred
preach.

If you have merit, you will sigh and
sob,

If you are backward, you might get a
job.

Out of caste, if you dare to wed, off

Your kith and kin will chop your head.

If you are honest, in north or in south,

You will live from hand to mouth.

If you are wily and your means sinister,

You are likely to become a chief
minister.

But remember the new maxim, my
lad,

Defection is good, conversion is bad.

❐

An Englishman, an American, and a

Sardarji were called upon to test 'a lie detector.

The Englishman said, 'I think I can empty twenty bottles of beer.'

BUZZZZZ went the lie detector.

'OK,' he said, 'Ten bottles.' And the machine was silent.

The American said, 'I think I can eat fifteen hamburgers.'

BUZZZZZ went the lie detector.

'All right, eight hamburgers.' And the machine was silent.

The Sardarji said, 'I think . . .'

BUZZZZZ went the machine!

❏

Santa saw that his friend Ram Lal was very depressed.

'What happened?' asked Santa.

'*Yaar*, I lost Rs 800 in a bet yesterday.'

'How come?'

'Well, yesterday, the one-day match between India and England was being shown live on TV. I bet Rs 500 that India would win, but I lost the bet.'

'But that's only Rs 500, where did the rest go?'

'*Yaar*, I bet on the highlights too!'

❏

Three men applied for the job of a detective: Santa from India, Marc Grayberg, a Jew, and Tom Silanti, an Italian.

The chief decided to ask each applicant just one question and base his decision upon the answer. When Grayberg arrived for his interview, the chief asked him, 'Who killed Jesus Christ?' He answered without hesitation, 'The Romans killed him.' The chief thanked him and he left.

When Silanti arrived for his interview, the chief asked him the same question. He replied, 'Jesus was killed by the Jews.' The chief thanked him too and he left.

Finally, Santa arrived for his interview and was asked the same question. He thought for a long time, before saying, 'Could I have some time to think about it?' The chief said, 'OK, but get back to me tomorrow.'

When Santa arrived home, his wife asked, 'How did the interview go?' Pat came the reply, 'Great, I got the job, and I'm already investigating a murder!'

❒

An Akali leader was fulminating against

the Congress. Addressing a crowded university meeting, he thundered, 'The Congress *wallahs* are all waters of the first rogue.'

The audience burst into laughter over his lapse of tongue. The Akali leader realized he had made a mistake. He joined the palms of his hands to ask for pardon, 'I am very sorry, it is a tongue of slip.'

This time the laughter was louder than before. The gentleman that he was, the Akali leader was genuinely contrite, 'You must pardon me. I am always limiting the cross.'

❐

Santa and Banta went fishing. They caught a lot of fish and returned to the shore.

Santa: 'I hope you remember the spot

where we caught all these fish.'

Barta: 'Yes, I marked X on the side of the boat to mark the spot.'

Santa: 'You idiot! How do we know we will get the same boat tomorrow?'

❐

Ujaagar's eldest daughter had been taken to the delivery room in a hospital and he was anxiously waiting outside when he heard the crying of a newborn babe. A few minutes later a nurse came out of the delivery room.

Ujaagar rushed up to her and enquired, 'Sister, am I a grandfather or a grandmother?'

❐

A tea party in honour of freedom fighters was in progress at Giani Zail Singh's house. Two other former Presidents, Neelam Sanjiva Reddy and R. Venkataraman were also present.

Suddenly a group of terrorists took over the party. They lined up all the three former Presidents for execution. As the firing squad got ready, Sanjiva Reddy yelled, 'Earthquake!' and escaped in the commotion that followed. The executioners got ready again, and as they took aim, Venkataraman shouted, 'Flood!' and he too escaped in the confusion. As the firing squad lined up for the third time, Zail Singh decided to try the same idea and yelled, 'Fire!'

❏

Two Pakistanis boarded a shuttle out of Washington for New York. One sat in the window seat, the other in the middle seat. Just before take-off, a fat, little Indian guy got on and took the aisle seat next to the Pakistanis.

He kicked off his shoes, wiggled his toes, and was settling in when the Pakistani in the window seat said, 'I think I'll go up and get a coke.'

'No problem,' said the Indian, 'I'll get it for you.'

While he was gone the Pakistani picked up the Indian's shoe and spat in it. When the Indian returned with the coke, the other Pakistani said, 'That looks good. I think I'll have one too.'

Again, the Indian obligingly went to fetch it, and while he was gone the second Pakistani picked up the other shoe and spat in it. The Indian returned with the

coke, and they all sat back and enjoyed
the short flight to New York.

As the plane was landing, the Indian
slipped his feet into his shoes and knew
immediately what had happened. 'How
long must this go on?' the Indian asked.
'This enmity between our people . . . this
hatred . . . this animosity . . . this spitting
in shoes and pissing in cokes?'

❏

Some Sikhs and Pakistanis were in
trenches facing one another. One Sikh
shouted, 'Mohammed *mia.*' A Pakistani
soldier stood up and shouted, 'Mohammed
mia ko kisne bulaya?' (Who called
Mohammed *mia?*) He got shot. Another
Sikh shouted, 'Azam Khan.' Azam Khan
stood up and said, '*Azam Khan ko kisne
bulaya*' and got shot.

The Pakistanis found it a great idea and decided to copy it. (It is in their genes to do everything after the Indians!) So a Pakistani soldier shouted, 'Swaran Singh.'

There was silence. After a couple of minutes one of the Sikhs shouted, 'Swaran Singh *ko kisne bulaya*?' (Who called Swaran Singh?)

A Pakistani soldier stood up—and got shot!

❐

Banta and his wife had a bitter quarrel and were yelling at each other.

'What do you think I am?' shouted Banta. 'You treat me like a dog.'

'I don't look upon you as a dog,' yelled back Banta's wife, 'but for God's sake stop barking at me.'

❐

Santa was playing rummy with his Alsatian dog. A passerby asked, 'Sardarji, can your dog recognize the cards?'

Replied Santa, 'Of course, but I win every time.'

The passerby asked, 'How do you manage to win all the time?'

Santa replied, 'You see, whenever he gets four-five jokers, his tail starts wagging. So I know it is time for me to pack up.'

❐

A journalist had done a story on gender roles in Kuwait several years before the Gulf War, and she had noted then that women customarily walked about ten feet behind their husbands. She returned to Kuwait a few years later and observed the men now walking several yards behind their wives.

She approached one of the women for an explanation.

'This is marvellous,' said the journalist. 'What enabled women here to achieve this reversal of roles?'

Replied the Kuwaiti woman, 'Landmines.'

❐

Why could Santa not make ice cubes?
Because he always forgot the recipe.

How did Santa try to kill the bird?
He threw it off a cliff.

What's the difference between Santa and a computer?
You have to punch information into a computer only once.

What do you get when you offer Santa a penny for his thoughts?

Change.

How do you keep Santa busy all day?
Put him in a round room and tell him
to find a corner.

And what does Santa come back and
tell you?
He tells you he found the corner!

What do you do when Santa throws a
pin at you?
Run like hell . . . he's got a hand
grenade in his mouth.

How do you make Santa laugh on
Saturday?
Tell him a joke on Wednesday.

What was Santa doing when he held
his hands tightly over his ears?
Trying to hold on to a thought.

❒

On a train from London to Manchester an American was telling off the Englishman sitting facing him in the compartment. 'You English are too stuffy. You set yourselves apart too much. Look at me . . . in me, I have Italian blood, French blood, a little Indian blood, and some Swedish blood. What do you say to that?'

The Englishman replied, 'Very sporting of your mother!'

□

A soldier who was on sentry duty was taken to the military hospital because he was suffering from chronic constipation.

When a visitor knocked on the door of his ward, he shouted: 'Who goes there? Friend or enema?'

□

A road sign on the way to Khandala from Bombay stated: 'When this sign is under water, the road is closed to traffic.'

❑

Sign on a narrow bridge:
Cars will not have intercourse on the bridge.

Medication:
Take three tablets a day until passing away.

In front of a chicken shop:
Eggs—extract of fowl.

Notice in a company's office:
Never argue with your boss—bosses are made to order!

Notice in a school corridor:
Exams in progress—please do not pass!

A Marwari from Jaipur went on his honeymoon to Kashmir alone. His wife had been there earlier.

❐

Teacher to a student: 'Tell me what important event took place in 1869?'

Student: 'Gandhiji was born that year.'

Teacher: 'Good! Now tell me what happened in 1872?'

Student: 'Gandhiji was three years old!'

❐

A lawyer and a blonde woman were sitting next to each other on a long flight. The lawyer leaned over to her and asked if she would like to play a fun game. The blonde declined and turned towards the window to catch forty winks. The lawyer persisted, saying that the game was really easy and a lot of fun. He explained, 'I ask you a question, and if you don't know the answer, you pay me, and vice-versa.'

Again, the blonde politely declined and tried to get some sleep. The lawyer made another offer: 'Okay, if you don't know the answer you pay me $5, but if I don't know the answer, I will pay you $50.'

The blonde agreed. The lawyer asked the first question. 'What's the distance from the earth to the moon?'

The blonde silently reached into her purse, pulled out a five-dollar bill, and handed it to the lawyer. Then she asked the lawyer, 'What goes up a hill with three legs, and comes down with four?'

The lawyer took out his laptop computer and searched all his references. He tapped into the airphone with his modem and searched the net. Frustrated, he sent e-mails to all his co-workers and friends. All to no avail. After over an hour, he gave up. He woke the blonde up and handed her $50. The blonde accepted it, then turned away to get back to sleep. The lawyer asked the blonde, 'Well, so what is the answer?'

Again, without a word, the blonde reached into her purse, handed the lawyer $5, and went back to sleep.

❐

Fed up of people making fun of him, Santa decided to change his religion. He became assistant to a priest in a church. One day the priest was called away for an emergency. Not wanting to leave the confessional unattended, he called Santa D'Costa (his new assistant) and asked him to cover for him. Santa told him he wouldn't know what to say, but the priest told him to stay with him for a little while and learn what to do.

Santa followed the priest into the confessional. A few minutes later a woman came in and said, 'Father forgive me for I have sinned.'

Priest: 'What did you do?'

Woman: 'I committed adultery.'

Priest: 'How many times?'

Woman: 'Three times.'

Priest: 'Say two Hail Marys, put $5 in the charity box, and sin no more.'

A few minutes later a man entered the confessional. He said, 'Father forgive me for I have sinned.'

Priest: 'What did you do?'

Man: 'I committed adultery.'

Priest: 'How many times?'

Man: 'Three times.'

Priest: 'Say two Hail Marys, put $5 in the charity box, and sin no more.'

Santa, a quick learner, told the priest that he understood the job and the priest could leave.

Santa D'Costa was now alone. A few minutes later another woman entered and said, 'Father forgive me for I have sinned.'

Santa: 'What did you do?'

Woman: 'I committed adultery.'

Santa: 'How many times?'

Woman: 'Once.'

Santa: 'Say two Hail Marys, put $5 in the charity box, and sin twice more!'

□

What is a Sikh scuba diver called?

Jal-Andhar-Singh.

What is the history of Punjab called?

Sarson-Da-Saga.

What would Punjabi International Airlines be called?

Kitthe Pacific.

What would Punjabi National Airlines be named?

Itthe Pacific.

What do you call a Sardar who drinks only beer?

Just-beer Singh.

What do you call a Sardar who has only one drink?

Just-one Singh.

What is a Sindhi lawyer called?

Case-wani.

What is a communist Sindhi called?

Lalwani.

What is a Sindhi who falls from the first floor called?

Thadani.

What is a Sindhi who falls from the thirtieth floor called?

Marjani.

What do you call a very rich Malayalee?
Million Iyer.

❐

Two germs met. 'Are you ill?' asked one, 'You look terrible.'

'Yes,' the other answered, 'I think I've caught an aspirin.'

❐

'Throw the baby down!' shouted the fireman to a woman on top of a blazing building.

'I won't!' she yelled back. 'You might drop him!'

'No, I won't!' he shouted back. 'I'm a professional goalkeeper!'

Reassured, the woman dropped her baby to the footballer, who immediately bounced the child three times and kicked him over the garden wall.

◻

The doctor told Banta that if he ran eight kilometres a day for 300 days, he would loose 34 kilos. At the end of 300 days, Banta called the doctor to report that he had lost the weight, but he had a problem.

'What's the problem?' asked the doctor.

'I am 2,400 kms from home,' replied Banta.

◻

There was this good samaritan barber in a city in the US. One day a florist went to him for a haircut. After the haircut when he wanted to pay, the barber replied, 'Thank you, but I cannot accept money from you; I am doing a community service.'

The florist was pleasantly surprised and went back happy. The next morning when the barber opened the shop, there was a thank you card with a dozen roses waiting at his door.

Next day, a cop went for a haircut and he also got the same reply from the barber: 'I am sorry, I cannot accept money from you; I am doing a community service.'

The cop was happy and left the shop. When the barber reached his shop the next morning, there was a thank you note and a dozen cookies waiting for him.

An Indian software engineer went for a haircut and when he wanted to pay the barber, he too got the same reply: 'I am sorry, I cannot accept money from you; I am doing a community service.'

The next morning when the barber went to open his shop, guess what he found there—

... a dozen Indians waiting for a free haircut.

❒

Wife: The two things I cook best are meatloaf and apple pie.'
Husband: 'Which is this?'

Newlywed: 'Do you want dinner?'
Spouse: 'Sure, what are my choices?'
Newlywed: 'Yes and no.'

First guy (proudly): 'My wife's an angel!'
Second guy: 'You're lucky, mine's still alive.'

On a summer holiday in New York Banta decided to visit a bar. At the bar, the man sitting on Banta's left told the bartender, 'Johnie Walker, single.' Then the man on his right ordered, 'Jack Daniels, single.' When the barman turned to Banta for an order, he said, 'Banta, married.'

❏

A regular brothel visitor got married one day and after his first night went straight to his best friend and started crying.

'What's the matter?' asked his friend.

'You know, *yaar*, as per my habit, I woke her up in the morning and gave her a hundred-rupee note,' he said.

His friend exclaimed, 'So what! Try to explain it to her, ask her to forget your past and lead a happy married life.'

'That's not the problem,' he said angrily, 'my wife gave me a fifty-rupee note back.'

❏

A Dutchman was explaining the red, white, and blue colours of his country's flag to an American tourist. 'It's symbolic of our taxes,' he said. 'We turn red when we talk about them, white when we figure them out, and blue when we pay them.'

The tourist answered, 'It's the same in America—only we see stars too!'

❏

'What kind of detective is Natha?'

'Well, once a burglar wearing calf-skin gloves robbed a safe. Natha took the

fingerprints and five days later arrested a
cow in Haryana.'

◻

A newly-opened clinic claimed:

We specialize in women and other
diseases.

A sign in a zoo showed that food prices
were soaring:

Please do not feed the animals. If you
have any suitable food, give it to the guard
on duty.

Seen painted on a T-shirt:

Dating is a hit-or-miss proposition—a
girl who doesn't become a hit, remains a
miss!

Notice outside an electronic shop:

Exchange everything for new—TV,

refrigerator, washing machine, etc. Bring along your wife—an excellent bargain.

❐

Cardinal Gracius was once invited to give the first holy communion in a church in Bombay. The parish priest had prepared the young children thoroughly on how to respond to the prayers during the Holy Mass. He had taught the children that the response to the Bishop's saying 'The Lord be with you' would be—'And also with you.'

As the Cardinal began the Holy Mass, he found that the mike was not working. He turned around to the parish priest and said, 'Something is wrong with the mike.'

The children, well trained as they were, answered in a loud voice: 'And also with you.'

She: 'Here's your ring back. I can't marry you because I love someone else.'

He: 'Who is he?'

She (nervously): 'You're not going to try to kill him?'

He: 'No, but I'll try and sell him the ring.'

❐

Banta went to his doctor with two red ears. The doctor asked him what had happened to his ears and he answered, 'I was ironing a shirt and the phone rang, but instead of picking up the phone I accidently picked up the iron and stuck it to my ear.'

'Oh, dear!' the doctor exclaimed in disbelief. 'But what happened to your other ear?'

'The scoundrel called back.'

When he came across a long procession of people led by a man with a dog, Santa asked the man, 'Who died?'

'My mother-in-law.'

'How?'

'The dog bit her.'

'May I borrow the dog?'

'Get in line.'

❐

Santa and Banta were having difficulty trying to unlock the door of their Mercedes with a coat hanger.

In an extremely frustrated tone Banta said, 'I can't seem to get this door unlocked.'

'Well, you would better hurry up and try a little harder. It has started raining and the top of the car is down!' replied Santa.

Indians have taken to St Valentine's day with zest. Here are some samples of messages which appeared in the newspapers that day.

A message read: 'Nearest, dearest, closest, sweetest, cutest, loveliest, hauntiest, tastiest, wittiest, crunchiest, *Jannu.* I just called to say I love you. Yours and only yours.'

Not to be outdone another gushed: 'Dearest Limpo, you are the most crunchiest, munchiest, loveliest, sensuous, wittiest, funniest, terrific guy I love. Lots lots, lots of love to Limpo.'

Still another message read. 'To Samta, my love, my life, my dream, my reality, my one and only wife, my best friend.'

And another: 'Dear Anju, God created U4 me but I think he 4 got 2 tell U, UR 2 sweet 2 B4 go 10.'

And what about this: *'Meri Idiotni,* I

believe in you and I love you. *Tumhara*
Idiot.'

☐

Brown sahibs have lots of fun spotting
out grammar and spelling bloomers on
hoardings, ads and brochures put out by
their countrymen whose command over
English is not as good as theirs. An
American friend, Leonard J. Baldgya of
the US Embassy has sent a short
compilation of items picked up by
American students in different parts of
Europe. They make as good reading as
our Hinglish:

In a Bucharest hotel lobby: 'The lift is
being fixed for the next day. During that
time we regret that you will be unbearable.'

In a Belgrade hotel elevator: 'To move
the cabin, push button for wishing floor. If

the cabin should enter more persons, each one should press a number of wishing floor. Driving is then going alphabetically by national order.'

In a hotel in Athens: 'Visitors are expected to complain at the office between the hours of 9 and 11 a.m. daily.'

In a Japanese hotel: 'You are invited to take advantage of the chamber-maid.'

In the lobby of a Moscow hotel across from a Russian orthodox monastery: 'You are welcome to visit the cemetery where famous Russian composers, artists, and writers are buried daily except Thursday.'

In an Austrian hotel catering to skiers: 'Not to perambulate the corridors in the hours of repose in the boots of ascension.'

On the menu of a Polish hotel: 'Salad, a firm's own make; limpid red beet soup with cheesy dumplings in the form of a finger; roasted duck let loose; beef rashers beaten up in the countrypeople's fashion.'

In a Bangkok dry cleaner's shop: 'Drop your trousers here for best results.'

Outside a Paris dress shop: 'Dresses for street-walking.'

Outside a Hong Kong dress shop: 'Ladies have fits upstairs.'

In an advertisement by a Hong Kong dentist: 'Teeth extracted by the latest Methodists.'

In a Czechoslovakian tourist agency: 'Take one of our horse-driven city tours—we guarantee no miscarriages.'

Detour sign in Kyushi, Japan: 'Stop— Drive Sideways.'

In a Swiss mountain inn: 'Special today—no ice cream.'

In a Bangkok temple: 'It is forbidden to enter a woman, even a foreigner, if dressed as a man.'

In a Tokyo bar: 'Special cocktail for

ladies with nuts.'

In a Copenhagen airline office: 'We take your bags and send them in all directions.'

In a Rome laundry: 'Ladies, leave your clothes here and spend the afternoon having a good time.'

A translated sentence from a Russian chess book: 'A lot of water has been passed under the bridge since this variation has been played.'

In a Rhodes tailor shop: 'Order your summers suit. Because is big rush we will execute customers in strict rotation.'

In an East African newspaper: 'A new swimming pool is rapidly taking shape since the contractors have thrown in the bulk of their workers.'

Advertisement for donkey rides in Thailand: 'Would you like to ride on your own ass?'

In the window of a Swedish furrier: 'Fur coats made for ladies from their own skin.'

Two signs from a Majorcan shop entrance:
'English well talking.'

'Here speeching American.'

From a brochure of a car rental firm in Tokyo: 'When passenger of foot heave in sight, tootle the horn. Trumpet him melodiously at first, but if he still obstacles your passage then tootle him with vigour.'

❏

'Take me to the tenth floor,' said Banta as he entered the lift of a high rise building. When the lift reached its destination, the liftman opened its gates and said, 'The tenth floor, *beta*.'

'Why did you call me *beta*?' demanded Banta. 'I am not your son.'

'I called you *beta* because I brought you up,' replied the liftman.

Poor man: 'Lord, is it true that to you a thousand years is like a second?'

God: 'Yes, that's true.'

Poor man: 'And is it also true that to you a thousand crores is like a paisa?'

God: 'Yes, that's so.'

Poor man: 'Then, Lord, could you give me a thousand crores?'

God: 'Yes, in a minute.'

□

A boy in love with a girl presented her with a lotus flower. In return the girl gave him a tight slap across his face. The boy was taken aback and asked, 'I gave you a flower and you paid me back in this way. Why?'

The girl replied, 'You gave me a *kamal* which is the emblem of the BJP and I gave you *haath* which is the emblem of the Congress party.'